THE EXPLOSION OF
BRITISH SOCIETY, 1914-62

Compare the health, the attitudes, and the opportunities of the man in the street today with those of his counterpart in 1914, barely making ends meet on thirty shillings a week. No doubt as to the explosive changes, for good or bad, which have taken place in British society in the intervening years.

This explosion was touched off by the First World War and has involved the interaction of many forces, social, economic, cultural, scientific, and political.

Interaction, that is the basic concern of the historian: films, novels, poems, pogo sticks, and bingo, as well as the major crises of war and peace, have all been woven into the pattern of this book.

But the two dominant themes in recent British history are the growth of social welfare and the expansion of science. Professional historians are still too reluctant to deal adequately with the impact of science on society. This book makes some attempt to redress the balance.

THE EXPLOSION OF BRITISH SOCIETY, 1914-62

ARTHUR MARWICK

A PAN ORIGINAL

A NEW BOOK WRITTEN SPECIALLY FOR
PAN BOOKS LTD : LONDON

First published 1963 by

PAN BOOKS LTD

8 Headfort Place, London, S.W.1

Printed in Great Britain by
Cox and Wyman Ltd., London, Fakenham and Reading

CONTENTS

ACKNOWLEDGEMENTS

I should like to express a personal debt to Miss
Sandra Muir and Mrs E. Thomas, who typed
parts of this book, and to Mlle Odette Furois and
Miss Heather Mackewn, who read it in typescript
or in proof.

Acknowledgements are due to Mr. Graham
Greene and William Heinemann Limited for permission to quote from *It's a Battlefield*, to Long-
mans, Green & Company Limited for permission to
quote from *Gentian Violet* by Edward Hyams, to
The Spectator for permission to quote from the
article by Mr Simon Raven, to Mr J. B. Priestley
and William Heinemann Limited for permission
to quote from *Three Men in New Suits*, to Mr
Lawrence Wright and Routledge and Kegan Paul
Limited for permission to quote from *Clean and
Decent*, and to Mr W. H. Auden and Faber &
Faber Limited for permission to quote three lines
from *Poems*.

INTRODUCTION: THE PATTERN OF
THE BOOK

THE search for historical watersheds is a notoriously unrewarding one. If not exactly a watershed, the First World War was certainly a steep and sharp waterfall in the course of British history. All the economic, social, cultural and political forces which have moulded twentieth-century Britain were already in flow before 1914, but the war accelerated them with such suddenness and turbulence that they were transformed on a gigantic scale.

Furthermore, the war hit British consciousness with traumatic force, leaving bitterness and cynicism in its train. In this sense it was immeasurably more shattering in its effects on British society than the Second World War: the thirties and forties were equipped with a knowledge of the horrors of total war unimagined by the relatively placid Edwardian and Georgian Britain. Each year from 1914 to 1918 twice as many combatants were killed compared with each single year from 1939 to 1945. The sacrifice seemed grossly unequal: while profiteering was rampant at home, civilians were not linked to the men in arms, as in the second war, through suffering the parallel menace of wholesale aerial bombardment. Bitterness, division, cynicism, were aggravated by growing doubts as to the competence of the military and political direction of the war.

In the long view Britain's reason for entering the fray in August, 1914, was to combat the challenge presented by Germany to what remained of the commercial and naval supremacy established during the reign of Queen Victoria. In the immediate view stood the threat of German domination of the European continent. The German violation of Belgian territory provided the actual *casus belli* for Britain, and served to rally British sentiment behind the Government. Clearly, however, no power was completely blameless in the series of events which led to hostilities – the division of Europe into two opposing camps, the arms race, and the German fear that she was being 'encircled'. The ranks of those who repudiated the pre-war diplomacy and called in question the whole necessity for British participation in the war gained increasing and influential strength after 1918. Here was a further factor in the war's legacy of doubt and challenge to established authority.

The thesis upon which this book is based, then, is as follows. So great was the impact of the war, both in bringing a final challenge to nineteenth-century absolutes and in transforming the social and economic structure of Britain, that the phase 1914 to 1920 can be described as one of 'explosion'. The exigencies of war forced the Government to assert greater control than ever before over a wide range of the community's activities. The rapid growth of collectivism, that is to say State interference in, and regulation of, economic and social matters, is one of the two basic themes in British history since 1914. The other theme is the advance of science, particularly in the sense of its increasing impingement on the ordinary life of the country; here, again, the First World War was of crucial importance.

Although the war ended in November, 1918, the post-war boom prolonged much of the wartime atmosphere till 1920. With the collapse of the boom, and the onset of the long depression which lasted till the Second World War, there was something of a retreat from the new developments of the war period. While the collectivist process was not completely halted, the politicians now concentrated on economy and retrenchment. In society as a whole the cynicism and scepticism to which we have referred took the form of a bitter-sweet irresponsibility and detachment from social and political issues. At the same time the interaction between science and society brought the first major stage towards the new social dominion of mass communications (broadcasting, film, and Press) which we know today. The rather unheroic twenties met their end in the great economic and political crisis of

1931; I have described the period from 1920 to 1931 as one of 'contraction'.

The great crisis did, however, force people to re-examine the lessons of the war. Although a time of continued industrial depression, the thirties was also the decade of deep social concern, of sharp political feeling, of 'commitment', and of 'planning'. There was still, as in the twenties, a lack of truly great political leadership – and this was to prove fatal in the context of gathering international tension, yet it was in the years between the great crisis and the outbreak of the Second World War that much of the fundamental thinking underlying the Welfare State of today was accomplished. This phase, then, I have described as one of 'expansion'.

The Second World War again brought the inevitable extension of State control. In addition, the immediate common danger engendered a powerful sense of community spirit, and brought to full fruition the stirrings of social conscience of the thirties. This time there was no retreat at the end of the war, so that the phase 1940 to 1950 was again one of 'explosion', culminating in the establishment of the Welfare State and full employment economy. After 1950 there were no further dramatic advances, but there was a fairly general acceptance among people of all political persuasions of the changes which had already taken place; this phase was one of 'consolidation'.

At the time of writing it appears as if this period of consolidation may be coming to an end, and that British society is about to embark on a further period of change. Whether this be so or not, there can be no doubt that the cumulative effect of the phasing described above has been one gigantic explosion, involving a great rise in living standards, great changes in cultural activities and social attitudes, and the reorganization of the political structure and reallocation of the centres of power in the community.

Note on Books

Writers and books on specific topics have been referred to in the course of the text.

The two main themes can be further explored in M. Bruce, *The Coming of the Welfare State*, and J. G. Crowther, *British Scientists of the Twentieth Century* (amplified by M. Gorham on *Broadcasting and Television*).

Three more general works should also be mentioned. First of all every student of the period owes a great debt to Professor C. L. Mowat's monumental *Britain Between the Wars*. On the same period, R. Graves and A. Hodge, *The Long Week-end*, despite occasional inaccuracies, is also extremely valuable. Henry Pelling's *Modern Britain 1885–1955* gives a very lucid outline, especially of the international and political background.

CHAPTER ONE

THE IMPACT OF THE WAR

ACCORDING to the 1911 census the population of Great Britain was 40·8 millions; the population of Ireland, still governed wholly from Westminster, had declined slightly over the previous ten years to just over 4 millions. The comparable figures for the United States and Germany, Britain's two strongest commercial rivals, were, respectively, 91·7 millions and 64·9 millions. The process of urbanization had been going on long enough for the pattern of town-living with which we are familiar today to have been well established. On average there were 373 Britons to every square mile (the German figure was 310); for England and Wales alone the average density was 618 per square mile. Politically Britain was almost, but not quite, a democracy; about 8 millions of her citizens had the vote.

Since 1898 the general price level had been rising, so that in the business world there was an atmosphere of optimism. But beneath the surface placidity there were elements of tension and change. On the one hand was the extravagance of high society, the lavish pageantry of the era of *My Fair Lady* and the colour of the Edwardian music hall (this was the hey-day of such great entertainers as Harry Lauder), on the other the miseries of the sweated trades, the growing militance of a working class hit by rising prices and finding the average 1914 wage of just over thirty shillings a week insufficient for the maintenance of a family, and the violence associated with the suffragettes, the struggle between the Lords and Commons, and the gathering conflict in Ireland. The elements of change can be seen in the important social reforms culminating in the

1911 National Insurance Act, in the rise of the cinema (there were 3,500 in 1914), and in the growing popularity among the well-to-do of the motor-car, of which there were 132,015 in 1914 – confined, however, to a speed limit of twenty miles per hour.

Edwardian Britain was groping towards many of the ordinary features of later twentieth-century British life:

Western civilization had at last made up its mind as to what form of bath it really wanted: a solo tub about 5 ft 6 ins. long, parallel-sided or slightly tapered, with a roll-rim and with taps attached to the bath itself. The large and growing demand made a cheap standard product practicable. Sheet metal, needing skilled handwork, went out of use. About 1910 the cast-iron single-shell bath, enamelled on the inside only, and either painted outside or cased in, was in quantity production at a price the masses could pay. (L. Wright, *Clean and Decent*, p. 237.)

Even so, as far as the working classes were concerned, conditions had not changed greatly since the turn of the century when Seebohm Rowntree, in a social survey of York, had found baths in working-class houses to be 'practically unknown'.

By 1914 the lounge suit was accepted dress for men, and off-the-peg tailoring was making for greater standardization throughout the social scale: a Royal Academician, in 1911, lamented the 'time when a duke could be recognized by his garb'. In part this development was attributed to the American influence, felt strongly for the first time by the cosmopolitan Edwardians. For all that, class distinctions were very sharp. *Punch* was still presenting beery-nosed, ill-clad proletarians oozing obsequious respect for the 'guv'nor'. Give the poor baths, many of their social superiors felt, and they would only put coal in them. Every middle-class household had its servants, most of whom, for their part, were only too conscious of their 'place' in the social hierarchy.

Extravagance and poverty, change and class consciousness; yet with the advent of war the country re-found its unity. It was in the years that followed that the real shocks came.

It would have been possible during the Napoleonic wars to lead an active social life and be only vaguely aware that Britain was engaged in a struggle for survival. But once the optimism of 1914 had vanished ('Business as usual' was the fatuous slogan of the first months), war rapidly dominated all aspects of social life. Shortages at home and in restaurants, queues for anything from coal to beer, rationing, and such austere dietary innovations as shepherd's pie ('But, mummy, it's a particularly nasty piece of shepherd', wept the little boy in the *Punch* cartoon) were regular features. The tenor of British life was disfigured by outcries against people with German-sounding names or German associations, however remote (the most eminent victims were Prince Louis of Battenberg, and Lord Haldane, who had been educated in Germany), by attacks on pacifists and war-resisters, and by periodic spy-scares.

More disruptive were the small-scale (and, in reality, rather ineffective) raids by German airships and, later, aeroplanes. Air Raid Precaution was left very much to local initiative, and to begin with tended to be much resented by the British public. The Chief Constable of Middlesbrough, for instance, reported on his attempts to enforce a 'black-out':

The general public did not take kindly to the enforcement of these Orders so far as house and shop lights were concerned, and the action of the Chief Constable was challenged by the Watch Committee. The majority of the members of the Committee at this period were against the action of the Chief Constable, but, before many months had passed, were absolutely in favour of the steps taken in the interests of the community. (*Middlesbrough's Effort in the Great War*, p. 126.)

However, it was the actual fighting of the war, in which over six million men directly participated, and the dreadful losses suffered at the front, which ate most deeply into the British consciousness. We must therefore glance at the main outlines of the military campaigns before we proceed to consider the long-term social and economic consequences of the war.

The British military leaders upon whom criticism was later heaped were Lord Kitchener at the War Office (till January, 1916), Sir John French, Commander in Chief of the British

Forces in France till 1915, Sir Douglas Haig who replaced him, and Sir William Robertson, Chief of the Imperial General Staff from 1915 till the last year of the war. The basic criticism of the generals concerns their out-dated belief in the value of mere numbers, and their resistance to technical innovation. As Liddell Hart has commented: 'There is only one thing harder than getting an old idea out of the military mind, and that is to get a new one in.' Despite the object lesson of the American Civil War, there was no appreciation of the over-riding supremacy of the machine-gun in trench warfare: 'a much over-rated weapon,' Haig called it. Similarly Kitchener wrote off the tank, which was to play a most important part in the Allies' final offensive, as 'a pretty mechanical toy'.

The war began with the Germans' well-planned scythe-sweep through the low countries, in face of which the French and the small British Expeditionary Force were forced to retreat. At the Battle of the Marne this movement was halted and the situation became stabilized as, it proved, it was to remain until the last months of the war: for almost four years the war in the west was fought on the trench barrier now established from Switzerland to the Channel. The paradox quickly emerged that the side which ventured upon the offensive almost invariably suffered heavier losses than the defence. Thus the Allied Autumn offensive of 1915 brought the total of casualties at the end of that year to two and a half million. Similarly the Spring offensive of 1917, upon which Haig insisted against Lloyd George's better judgement, brought only terrible losses in the swamps of Passchendaele. In the end the German advances of early 1918, at first fraught with danger for the Allies, but never successfully exploited, brought greater gains to the Allies than had any of their own offensives.

For most of the men who fought in it, then, the First World War meant a constant and seemingly fruitless agony of mud and blood almost impossible to describe to those at home. 'There are some things better left undescribed . . . perhaps in the afterwards, when time has somewhat deadened matters, you will hear of them', wrote one young private from the front line. (*Letters of a Durisdeer Soldier*, p. 84.)

British troops were concentrated on the Western Front because this was where the influential generals were serving. But war, of course, was being waged in several other theatres. At the beginning of 1915 there was a strong body of opinion in the British Cabinet in favour of opening a front in the Balkans. The 'Easterners' – Churchill at the Admiralty, Lloyd George, and Hankey, the Secretary of the War Council, were the most influential of them – met with strong opposition from the 'Westerners', the advocates of more and still more concentration on the Western Front. When finally, in March, 1915, a naval expedition was dispatched to the Dardanelles it was starved of the full resources needed to guarantee the successful opening of a new front, and it lacked a clear definition of objectives. The actual operation was conducted with monumental feebleness and eventually petered out.

At sea, Britain, after some initial losses, succeeded by the end of 1914 in bottling up the German fleet. This left the way clear, on the one hand, for British successes overseas. On the other hand it turned the Germans towards the use of submarine warfare (with, as we shall see, momentous consequences for British society as a whole). The first submarine campaign was not particularly effective, but it did serve as a magnet for the wrath of the United States, hitherto directed against the British interference with neutral shipping rights: American opinion took a decisive swing with the sinking of the Cunard ship *Lusitania* on 7th May, 1915.

It was only after the naval encounter known as the Battle of Jutland that the submarine menace became really serious. Jutland itself was inconclusive, but it served to arouse doubt as to the competence of the British Admiral, Sir John Jellicoe. By April, 1917, one out of four ships leaving the British Isles never came home: the half-dozen submarines operating in the Channel approaches were doing a deadly business. Hankey and Lloyd George, now Prime Minister, wanted to adopt the convoy system in an attempt to surmount this dire threat to the nation's economic survival; Jellicoe and the admirals would not hear of it. But Lloyd George got his way: as a result the shipping loss dropped by two thirds. By the end of the year new methods of anti-submarine warfare evolved by British scientists had practically brought the danger to an end.

Meantime Germany's indiscriminate use of the submarine weapon had brought America into the war (6th April, 1917). The American force was at first of little practical military value, but her entry was of great importance to the Allies in three respects: it gave their morale a powerful boost; it provided them with direct economic assistance; and it involved a significant tightening in the economic stranglehold which Britain was exerting on the Central Powers.

After the collapse of the German advances of the Spring of 1918, the Americans played an important part in driving back the exhausted German forces. It was the second Battle of the Marne which revealed that the ascendancy had definitely passed to the Allies. A series of local offensives in August and September led on to the Allied Grand Offensive. Its progress was far from grand, but events on other battlefields hastened the end. On 31st October the Turkish Empire collapsed, then, true to the ironical pattern of this war, Austria broke herself in a fatal offensive on the Italian front, and, on 4th November, concluded an armistice with the Italians.

Meanwhile, although the German armies were withdrawing in good order, the country itself had been brought to starvation point by the Allied blockade. Following the outbreak of revolution, armistice terms were signed on 11th November. There had still been no conclusive military engagement, hence the later German legend of the 'stab in the back'. It was a final irony of the war that, after all the concentration on the Western Front, the final victory came through, not military, but economic pressure.

In achieving this pressure Britain had herself undergone what in effect amounted to a revolution in her economic structure. The slow but steady advance of collectivism, that is to say State interference in, and regulation of, social and economic life, had been apparent since the late nineteenth century. But under the disciplines of war collectivism was given a brief and far from omnicompetent reign till 1920; thereafter, although there was immediate retreat, the lessons of the war economy could never be completely forgotten.

The two big emergencies which brought about the first advances in large-scale State control were the need for munitions and the threat to the country's food supply, rendered especially serious by German submarine operations. After a Ministry of Munitions had been founded, a comprehensive control of all the war industries was built up through various Government Committees and Acts of Parliament. In the case of the food shortage the Government had deliberately to reverse the trend of forty years whereby Britain had been steadily converting her arable land to pasture, so that on the eve of the war she was importing four-fifths of her wheat. In December, 1916, committees were established in every county with compulsory powers in regard to sowing of crops, ploughing of pasture, and so on. The Corn Production Act of 1917 gave the farmers guaranteed minimum prices, unnecessarily as it proved, and, more significantly, gave the farm labourers guaranteed minimum wages. A Ministry of Food was set up in 1917, when an attempt was also made to enforce control of retail prices; ration cards did not come in till early 1918.

To get the most out of the railways, they were run as a unified system under the Railway Executive Committee, which consisted of the general managers of the principal private companies of pre-war days. A Select Committee of 1918 recommended that there should be no return to the 1914 position, and suggested that ultimately there should be complete unification. Steps in this direction were the establishment in 1919 of a Ministry of Transport, and the Railways Act of 1921, which, like a giant sausage machine, swallowed up the hodge-podge of one hundred and twenty existing companies and churned them out as the 'Big Four' – the London, Midland and Scottish, the London and North Eastern, the Great Western, and the Southern. The coal industry, similarly, was put under State management for as long as hostilities lasted. At the end of the war the Sankey Commission, by a majority, recommended nationalization, but the Government, unwisely as it proved, ignored this verdict. As a last word on the progress of the theory of State control of industry, it may be mentioned that during the war even the nationalization of the liquor trade was seriously mooted, for drink, it was felt, was impairing the efficiency of the war effort.

Two of the greatest articles of mid-Victorian faith had been Free Trade and Free Currency (that is to say currency which is entirely open to the fluctuations of the gold market, and completely free from State management). Although together these had been an important impetus behind mid-Victorian prosperity, since 1880, Free Trade, at least, had come under fire. But on the outbreak of war it was actually orthodox currency policy which was the first casualty. The Currency and Bank Notes Act of 6th August, 1914, authorized the Bank of England to expand the issue of notes not backed by gold (the Fiduciary Issue), and made provision for the printing by the Treasury of one pound and ten shilling notes. In effect the country was off the Gold Standard. Naturally inflation followed: the purchasing power in circulation between 1914 and 1920 increased by 125 per cent. At the end of the war the Cunliffe Committee, appointed by the Treasury, recommended the amalgamation of the Bank of England and the Treasury. Although it also called for deflation and a return to the Gold Standard (with implications which we shall discuss in a later chapter), it did not visualize an early return to an internal gold circulation. In fact the gold sovereign and half-sovereign had gone for good, to be replaced entirely by the paper currency with which we are familiar today, save that in 1927 the printing of the notes was handed over by the Treasury to the Bank of England.

The first breach in Free Trade was opened in 1915 when the McKenna Duties imposed a 33⅓ per cent tariff on 'luxury' imports, including motor-cars. Key industries – drugs and scientific instruments, for example – were 'safeguarded'. The breach was maintained in the Safeguarding of Industries Act of 1921.

As was to be expected the main financial burden of the war was shouldered on posterity, the National Debt leaping from

£650 millions to £7,000 millions. But the heavy expenditure of war did bring about a substantial movement towards a progressive tax structure. From ninepence in the pound, income tax rose to six shillings. Super tax, and excess profits duties were also imposed, although the latter, without effective price control, were something of a farce. These fiscal innovations must have brought the custodian of Victorian financial orthodoxy, William Ewart Gladstone, bounding from his grave, for successive Chancellors of the Exchequer in the years after the war, as we shall see, were to act as if Gladstone's ghost were standing at their shoulder.

Rigid State direction in time of total war was not without its evil effects. The Defence of the Realm Acts, immediately and widely known, with a sort of wry affection, as 'Dora', were often harsh, perhaps even brutal, as they affected individuals. Yet to many people of progressive sympathies the war seemed a triumph of State planning. After the armistice there was a general movement for radical elements towards the Labour party, and a certain Major Clement Attlee (now Earl Attlee), for example, felt confirmed in his earlier attachment to Socialism. The advance of collectivism is one of the major themes of this book; we shall see it at work in many of the other forces of change accelerated by the war. It is to them that we must now turn.

CHAPTER TWO

THE FORCES OF CHANGE

THE nineteenth century, in a historical cliché, was the century of science. So is the twentieth century, only more so. The five governing advances of twentieth-century science have been the development of nuclear physics, the theory of relativity, the new sciences of biochemistry, in which the British pioneer was Frederick Gowland Hopkins (1861–1947), and genetics – the word was coined in 1905 by William Bateson – and the new psychology based particularly on the discoveries of Freud.

At first the war seemed to pose an obstacle to the progress of British science. J. J. Thomson (1856–1940), Cavendish professor at Cambridge, who, in 1897, had conclusively proved the existence of the electron, had passed the peak of his powers as an experimental scientist. His great protégé, Ernest Rutherford, a New Zealander (like Thomson, he was of Scottish descent), had already in 1911 constructed a model of the atom. In 1915 he turned, not very fruitfully, to the problem of submarine detection; in the same year one of his most capable assistants was killed at Gallipoli. Rutherford returned to his lonely laboratory in Manchester, and in the closing months of the war he achieved one of the crucial developments of modern science – the artificial disintegration of the atom. In 1918 he succeeded Thomson at Cambridge and thereafter he had working around him at the Cavendish laboratory such distinguished younger men of British science as E. V. Appleton, P. M. S. Blackett, and J. D. Cockcroft.

The smashing of the atom required physical apparatus on an engineering scale; thus for reasons of expense alone physics had to come down from the ivory tower into the commercial world of the electrical engineering industry. In the other aspects of the new industrial revolution in which science itself became an industry, asserting an increasing sway over the activities of the community, the war was the turning-point. The exposure of Britain's dangerous nakedness in the production of explosives, drugs, dyes, and scientific instruments forced the Government, through the creation of the Department of Scientific and Industrial Research, into the realms of science. Before the war a Cambridge professor could maintain, 'scientific research is a proper occupation for the leisure of an English gentleman'. Now the industrial side of science, particularly in chemicals, described by Professor J. D. Bernal (*Science in History*, p. 569) as 'the central industry in modern civilization', expanded rapidly. In 1918 the National Union of Scientific Workers was founded, and in the following years industry gave employment to a growing army of scientific researchers.

A noteworthy and representative figure is W. C. Pye, who, from being head of the Cavendish workshops, became a manufacturer in the nascent radio industry. The sending of signals by wireless had been demonstrated in London as far back as 1896 by the Italian inventor, Guglielmo Marconi. Oddly enough, till the war, wireless was thought of solely as a means of conveying information. It was Arthur Burrows, employed by the Government in collecting, editing and distributing to Government Departments the wireless propaganda of the Central Powers, who was the first in this country to visualize the use of wireless for entertainment broadcasts (A. Briggs, *Mass Entertainment*, p. 25). In the early twenties this medium became established as one of the most important of the 'mass communications' which have played a decisive part in shaping contemporary British society.

As important, perhaps, was the stimulus given by the war to developments in the internal combustion engine. The change, in the post-war years, from luxury to family status in the motor-car, and the territorial conquests of the motor-bus, have had ramifications all through British society. Isolated villages were brought into the orbit of centralized British life. New industrial centres, new residential areas, new roads (followed by new methods of outdoor advertising) were built. The mass production techniques pioneered in the United States by Henry Ford poured like a great tidal wave first through the motor-car industry then through the British economy as a whole, bearing on its crest new consumer goods, radio sets and pre-packed foods. If air raids were of little improtance in the war, aeroplanes did show their potential when used for reconnaissance. In the years after the war there came the first advances in civil aviation as a commercial venture.

The war gave a mighty push to the sciences; in the arts it had the effect of destroying for good the old canons which had been crumbling since the end of the previous century. Already George Bernard Shaw and John Galsworthy had brought a new realism and social purpose into the theatre. In his novel, *Ann Veronica* (1906), H. G. Wells had given flesh and words to the 'new woman' of the twentieth century, who explained:

Old-fashioned people . . . know right from wrong; they had a clear-cut religious faith, that seemed to explain everything. We haven't. I haven't, anyhow. And there's no good pretending there is one when there isn't.

Roger Fry, the distinguished art critic, had introduced the latest trends in French painting to the British public, though the British public showed little inclination to shake hands with the Post-impressionist devil. Now the horrors of war turned the modern movement in the arts into the channels of disillusionment. The younger artists and poets, particularly, felt the impact. Wyndham Lewis was already producing his Vorticist paintings when the war broke out, but the first important work of C. R. W. Nevinson, the Nash brothers, Stanley Spencer, and others, was a direct expression of the horrors and desolation of modern war: 'the most authoritative and concentrated utterance of war in the history of painting,' Sickert said of Nevinson's 'Mitrailleuse'.

On a less elevated, but socially more extensive plain, one might note the year 1915 as the turning point in the development of the film (another potential medium of 'mass communication') as a popular art form. In that year the troops at the front gave their overwhelming endorsement to the filmed antics of Charlie Chaplin.

The relevance of the arts to society as a whole depends very much upon the level of education in that society. It could not honestly be said that the British in 1914 were a well-educated nation. By 1918, however, it was felt that the elementary system had proved itself in the country's sorest trial. Fisher's Education Act of that year, though never put properly into operation, was designed in part to reinforce that system, and can be taken as a further symptom of the collectivist conscience of the war era. Another pre-war black spot which aroused concern was housing. Out of the old Local Government Board there was created, in 1918, a new Ministry of Health which, through the Act associated with Dr Addison, the first Minister, became responsible for a great sector of the nation's homes.

There were two broad forces of change dating from the late nineteenth century which had an obviously adverse effect on British society, and which were greatly aggravated by the war. The first to be considered is the declining birth rate. In 1914 the excess of births over deaths per thousand of the population of England and Wales stood at the low figure of 9·8; and in 1918 it had, for obvious reasons, dropped to 0·4. Although there was a brief 'baby boom' after the armistice, the slaughter of potential fathers in the war was irrevocable; nor could the spread of contraceptive techniques, encouraged during the war for prophylactic purposes, be resisted. The war, in fact, sounded the final death knell to the large family of Victorian times. Britain did not suffer from a 'lost generation' to the extent that France or the new Yugoslavia did, but, taking a wide perspective, the figures show that an annual increase in the population of around one per cent before the war became less than half of one per cent in the inter-war years. Thus the population became older; by the 1930's younger political leaders of quality were to be few and far between.

The decline of British industry in face of foreign competition had been a worrying feature of economic life since the 1870's. Although the effects were masked by the intensive industrial effort induced by the war itself, the interruption of trade held the seeds of disaster. Underdeveloped countries, hitherto fine markets for Britain, were forced to develop and adapt their own resources: at the end of the war they had ceased to be markets. Hence the British cotton industry, pride of mid-Victorian Britain, received blows from which it never recovered. British coal exports had reached their peak in 1913: such prosperity never returned. The exigencies of war forced the United States and Japan to a great expansion of their shipping resources. When the war and post-war boom collapsed in 1920, it became clear that the world had too many ships for its needs. The scene was set for the inter-war depression in Britain's basic industries.

To set against this tale of decline and woe we have the story of the dramatic advance of two important segments of the community. In the end the rise of the working class and the rise of the female sex were to prove infinitely more important in the explosion of British society than the two forces we have just been discussing.

From the formation of the 'model' trade unions in the 1850's the march of labour had been an increasingly important feature in British history up to 1914. The years immediately preceding the war had been years of great industrial unrest and even violence. With the outbreak of war the trade union leadership proclaimed an industrial truce. The Government, for its part, was forced to recognize the vital part the working class had to play in the war effort. The enforcement of arbitration involved an unprecedented recognition of the rights and status of labour.

Two troublesome areas resisted the cessation of normal trade union activity: South Wales and Clydeside. A strike of the South Wales miners in 1915 brought them almost all of their demands: their contribution to the war effort was too important for the Government to waste time in attempting coercion. On Clydeside a movement of discontent with the formal agreements between Government and trade union leadership spread through the engineering shops. The centre-pins of the movement were the shop stewards – the beginning of a process which has brought these officers, chosen by the men and serving with them on the shop floor, in and out of the public eye ever since. The Clyde Workers' Committee had the support of both revolutionary elements and of pacifists and democrats in the Independent Labour Party. But the entire labour movement on the Clyde was tarred with the brush of 'Red Clydeside'. After the serious strikes of 1916 a number of leaders were deported – among them David (later Lord) Kirkwood, who thus, somewhat undeservedly, gained the reputation of being an extremist. The Socialist weekly, *Forward*, also incurred official displeasure when it published an article beginning:

The best paid munitions worker in Britain, Mr Lloyd George (almost £100 per week), visited the Clyde last week in search of adventure. He got it . . .

The influence of the war upon the advance of the Labour movement can be seen in the trade union membership figures. From 4 millions in 1913, these rose to $6\frac{1}{2}$ millions in 1918, and $8\frac{1}{4}$ millions in 1920. In the trade union world, too, was to be found a counterpart of the industrial combination which had been steadily displacing the mid-Victorian ideals of private enterprise and unlimited competition. At the close of the war a number of new trade union giants emerged: the Iron and Steel Trades Confederation in 1917, the Amalgamated Engineering Union in 1920, and the Transport and General Workers Union in 1921. Finally, the new-found sense of purpose in the unions gained expression in the creation of the General Council of the TUC in place of the old Parliamentary Committee.

The activities of the militant suffragettes just before the war had thrown a dramatic light on the 'Women's Movement' which had actually been on the march since the 1820's. In the first months of the war the women's contribution to the national effort seemed to be confined to the handing out of white feathers to all young men still to be found skulking in civilian clothes. But from 1915 women were to be found playing full parts in the land army, in munition works, as lorry-drivers, as WAACs, or as WRENs. It was no longer possible to deny their worth to the community. After all the absurdity and tragedy of the suffragette movement, the Act of 1918 giving women over thirty the vote passed unresisted into law.

But women gained far more than political rights. For the first time they were earning good wages, and they had freedom. Before the war sexual liberty had been just permissible for the male: now official opinion came very near to condoning any consolation which might be offered to war heroes briefly returned from the trenches. The change in status was reflected in a change of dress. The pre-war skirt length which reached to the ground was much too hampering for the masculine activities which women undertook. Hence by the middle of 1915 the skirt had crept up to a position just below the calf: this was a revolutionary change which has never been reversed. For moral support under the stress of war there appeared for the first time in 1916 'the new undergarment which takes the place of the old-fashioned camisole', the brassiere.

CHAPTER THREE

THE POLITICIANS, THE WAR, AND IRELAND

IN politics, as elsewhere, the war, by bringing to crisis point a number of problems long in existence, helped to set the scene which has endured to our own day. The three topics to be considered here are the age-old tragedy of Ireland, the collapse of the historic Liberal party, and the rise of the Labour party. Taken together the last two in a sense represent the growing currency of the doctrines of collectivism at the expense of the older ideal of unrestricted competition. As for Ireland, it was Britain's Algeria: no honest account of the development of British society could omit a reference to this gaping hole in the armour of British democracy.

The core of Ireland's tragedy lay in its close proximity, yet utter dissimilarity, to Great Britain. Because of its very nearness the British politician knew no more of the particular social and economic structure of Ireland than the average Londoner knows of the Tower of London. Since the end of the century the Conservatives had followed an ambitious land reform policy designed to kill Home Rule with kindness. The Irish land problem was solved; but the Home Rule movement gained revolutionary intensity for it is a truism that it is just at the point when material conditions are on the upward turn that a revolutionary movement achieves its most dangerous dimensions. So it was with Ireland in the first decade of the twentieth century, when the Sinn Fein party was founded.

The drama reached its penultimate stages just before the War with the formation in Ireland of two rival armed bands. In the north the Ulster Volunteers pledged themselves to fight the Home Rule Bill which Asquith's Liberal Government was then piloting through the House of Commons and which, had war not intervened, should have become law in 1914. The Ulster card was thought to be a trump, for it was widely believed that without the economic wealth of Belfast, Ireland could not stand alone. In the south a ready reply had come in the establishment of the Irish Volunteers. Bonar Law, the leader of the Conservative opposition at Westminster, revealed a surprising disregard for constitutional propriety in giving his blessing to the preparations of the Ulster Unionists, who were vigorously led by a Dublin lawyer, Sir Edward Carson.

The weaknesses of the party in power at Westminster, the Liberals, were not readily apparent. But many of their essentially mid-Victorian articles of faith were ill-adapted to the cut-throat world of the twentieth century. They had already suffered one serious split over the 1886 Home Rule Bill, when most of their wealthiest support had gone over to the Conservatives. They had failed to make any appeal to the newly emergent suburban lower middle class of imperialist and, therefore, Conservative sympathies. Finally, with the twentieth century had come the Labour party, which although in 1914 still tied to one at least of the Liberal apron strings, was a potential rival for the progressive or working-class vote. The Liberals had won a sweeping victory in the 1906 general election, but much of their reform programme was vitiated by a hostile House of Lords intoxicated with its own reactionary exuberance, and their great majority was eaten away in the two general elections of 1910. On the other hand the Liberals did have to their credit Lloyd George's social reforms, and the Parliament Act of 1911, which curbed the powers of the House of Lords.

When war was declared the Cabinet, save for two ultra-Gladstonians, who resigned, stood behind Asquith and his Foreign Secretary, Grey. The Conservatives offered whole-hearted support, and the Irish Nationalists, under Redmond, a more qualified support. Ramsay MacDonald, chairman of the Parliamentary Labour party, opposed the war: but MacDonald had misjudged the temper of his party which proved to be overwhelmingly behind the war effort, and he himself went into the political wilderness with a group of more extreme opponents of the war, centred in the Independent Labour Party (ILP), then an autonomous body within the federal structure of the Labour party. With the agreement of the major parties, an electoral truce prevailed till the end of the war.

The Conservatives understood that Asquith would be dropping the bitterly contested Home Rule Bill. But Asquith, under pressure from the Nationalists, decided upon its enactment forthwith, with a proviso that it should not become law till the end of the war. The Conservatives, whom Asquith mocked as 'middle-aged gentlemen trying to look like early French revolutionaries in the tennis court', then marched out of the Chamber. This ended any immediate prospect of a coalition, and the political direction of the war rested, for the time being, in the hands of Asquith, Kitchener, and the First Lord of the Admiralty, Winston Churchill.

The first Coalition did not come till May, 1915. It was then necessitated, basically, by the crisis at the Admiralty over the unfortunate Dardanelles expedition. Churchill, anyway, was intensely disliked by the Conservatives, whom he had forsaken some years before, and his transfer to the Duchy of Lancaster became imperative. Balfour took his place, while Bonar Law came in in the rather inferior position of Colonial Secretary. The new Munitions Ministry went to the energetic Lloyd George who was able to attend to the shell shortage which had been a minor feature of the Cabinet crisis. Of great political significance was the inclusion of a Labour minister, Arthur Henderson, at the Board of Education. Asquith considered getting rid of Kitchener who had proved unequal to his tasks, but decided that his prestige value with the public was too high. This problem was solved later in the year by retaining Kitchener as a figurehead, but giving the real power to the new Chief of the Imperial General Staff, Sir William Robertson. The way was now clear, after this period of unsettlement, for the control of the war to pass to the generals; and throughout 1916 Haig and Robertson were the dominating figures. In June, 1916, Kitchener was drowned at sea: for his colleagues it was a blessed release.

Three problems troubled the domestic front in 1916. First, there was increasing criticism of what was held to be weak direction of the war on the part of Asquith. Secondly the insatiable demands of the Western Front gave pressing reality to the question of military conscription, long held to be against Britain's finest traditions. Thirdly, the Irish question erupted in the Dublin Easter Rising: with this we shall deal at the end of the chapter.

The Conservatives were the warmest supporters of conscription. Kitchener had at first been against the idea, and had, instead, with the aid of the celebrated posters, recruited a vast volunteer army of half a million. The greatest recruiting sergeant of the First World War was Horatio Bottomley, one of the few truly Dickensian villains to appear in modern British history; Bottomley was editor of *John Bull*, and a master of hypocrisy, jingoism, and financial malpractice. His final exposure and downfall came, as it came to Uriah Heep, with dramatic suddenness: but that was not till the 1920's.

Volunteer recruitment had been followed in the Autumn of 1915 by the inadequate system of 'attestation', which, despite promises to the contrary, was followed by universal conscription in May, 1916. Although previously it had expressed opposition, official Labour acquiesced with remarkable readiness. There was, however, a hard core of resistance, based on various ethical and political grounds. The Government did at least have the conscience to set up tribunals to consider cases of conscientious objection to military service, though many of these were farcical, or perhaps tragical, in operation. Conscientious objection, focused in the No Conscription Fellowship under the chairmanship of Clifford Allen, was a political force in the first war in a sense that it was not in the second. An important proportion of the later leadership of the Labour party spent the First World War in H.M. prisons. It is no surprise to learn that the old Labour stalwart (played by Stanley Holloway) in *No Love for Johnnie*, and Johnnie's own father, were conscientious objectors together.

Despite the mounting criticism, Asquith was fairly safe as long as there was no agreement between his two greatest potential rivals, Lloyd George and Bonar Law. He did, however, have powerful enemies in Carson, Lord Northcliffe, the owner of both *The Times* and the *Daily Mail*, and Max Aitken (soon created Lord Beaverbrook), the Canadian business man who had just acquired the *Daily Express*. Aitken it was who succeeded in overcoming Bonar Law's distrust of the 'Welsh Wizard'. Lloyd George, at first, wished to see the establishment of a small committee under his chairmanship entirely devoted to the prosecution of the war; Asquith would retain the name, and the domestic functions, of Prime Minister. While the Press skilfully played the Lloyd George game, Asquith, misadvised by his friends, broke off the negotiations which Lloyd George had initiated. The junction between Lloyd George and Bonar Law was decisive, and in December a new Coalition under the former was formed: whatever the rights and wrongs of the Cabinet crisis, there can be no doubt that Lloyd George was far better fitted than Asquith for firm direction of the war. The Press lords, perhaps, had played a bigger part than ever before, or ever since, in breaking and making a Cabinet; but in the end their influence was no more than marginal.

From the political point of view the crisis marked the second and fatal split in the Liberal party; its most brilliant figure was now leading a Government whose composition was overwhelmingly Conservative. From the constitutional point of view it brought two important developments. Lloyd George merged the War Council and the Cabinet into a small War Cabinet of himself, Bonar Law, Curzon, Henderson, and Milner, all, save for Bonar Law, who was Chancellor of the Exchequer, free from departmental duties. The other important development was the creation of a Cabinet Secretariat under Sir Maurice Hankey, whose brain was the most fertile and efficient in the whole British war effort. Now, for the first time, there was a proper record of Cabinet decisions. (The story of how, under the old régime, Asquith's inquiry after a Cabinet meeting, 'That's decided, then?' was met by Carson's reply, 'Yes, Prime Minister, but *what* have we decided?', is well known.)

The new Cabinet was soon faced with the necessity for taking a decision upon Haig's proposed Passchendaele offensive. Smuts was the only member definitely in favour, but the rest of the Cabinet were overborne by the military advisers: so much for Lloyd George's hope for strong political control. With the expensive failure of the offensive, Lloyd George was moved to adopt the device of starving the Western Front of men; this, obviously, left him open to criticism, especially with the mounting of the German offensive in March, 1918. The Prime Minister moved closer to the control he sought when he succeeded in bringing back Churchill as Minister of Munitions, and in replacing Sir William Robertson with Sir Henry Wilson. The latter move, and the weakening of the Western Front, provided the basis for an attack on the Government by Sir Frederick Maurice, with which Asquith, rather unwisely, associated himself. In the 'Maurice Debate' of 8th May, 1918, Lloyd George won a resounding success, endorsed by 293 votes to 106: politically the debate was of importance in separating out the Lloyd George sheep from the Asquithian goats in a bitterly divided Liberal party.

Political divergence of a more fundamental character emerged on the periphery of the charmed circle of Cabinet government. Lloyd George and the Conservatives were aiming simply at a total and unconditional defeat of the enemy. But by 1916 the ranks of the few who had opposed Britain's entry into the war, consolidated in 1915 in the Union of Democratic Control, which linked radicals like E. D. Morel, who was secretary, and Liberals like C. P. Trevelyan, with Labour men like MacDonald, were reinforced by other figures who believed that the time was ripe for a declaration of peace aims and an attempt at a negotiated peace: the most prominent, perhaps, was Lord Lansdowne, 'the last great Whig', and violent opponent of Home Rule. External factors which accelerated the tendency were the idealistic pronouncements of President Wilson of the United States, and the rapidly changing situation in Russia. Henderson came down in favour of a peace initiative through an international Socialist and Labour Conference, which was to be held at Stockholm. It was on this issue that

Henderson, after suffering the indignity of a long wait on the doormat outside the Cabinet room, was forced out of the War Cabinet. His place was taken by a much more docile Labour leader, Barnes. The various pressures did squeeze from Lloyd George, in January, 1918, an extremely vague statement of war aims. In fact, negotiation was even less acceptable to the German Government than it was to the British.

There was a strong feeling in political circles in 1918 that a general election was overdue: the new Representation of the People Act had given the vote to all men over twenty-one, and (save for a small property qualification) to all women over thirty, thus adding about 8 million new voters. And the existing parliament had, after all, been in existence since 1910. As the war came to its victorious close, Lloyd George and Bonar Law struck a bargain whereby the Coalition was to continue in being: Coalition candidates, distinguished, basically, by their conduct in the Maurice debate, were to receive a letter of endorsement, characterized by Asquith with topical sarcasm (rationing had recently been introduced) as a 'coupon'. Hence this, the second 'Khaki Election' in the country's history is alternatively known as the 'Coupon Election'. (Interestingly, Colonel Josiah Wedgwood, who shortly joined the Labour party, was, without willing it, allotted a coupon for his war service.)

Blinded by the jingoistic dusts thumped up by the politicians in the triumphant aftermath of war, the electorate voted the Coalition back into office with the crushing total of 474 seats (338 Conservatives, 136 Liberals). The free Liberals won only 26 seats, Asquith himself being defeated. They had been overtaken by Labour, who now had the – still modest – total of 59, though the two great pre-war leaders, MacDonald and Snowden, had been punished for their opposition to the war by the loss of their seats.

Under the leadership of the stolid Fifeshire miner, Adamson, and, subsequently, of the more competent, but not very inspired Clynes, Labour did not make as much as it might have done of its new opportunities. None the less, with the industrial developments already discussed, with the participation of

Labour leaders in the Coalition Governments, and with the accession of a large number of Liberals, on both internationalist and economic grounds, the advance of the Labour party must be accounted a major political consequence of the war. This advance was recognized in 1918 by the adoption of a new Party Constitution which in effect changed the Labour party from a loose federation into a monolithic mass party, open for the first time to individual members.

A second consequence was the riveting on the country during the vital years of post-war reconstruction of a heavily rightist Government, backed by a parliament 'of hard-faced men who looked as if they had done well out of the war'. One of the greatest political figures of modern times was to lead one of the worst Governments in the country's history. This Government was quickly to find itself involved in bloody civil war in Ireland, to which we must again turn.

Ireland

The advent of war had two important effects on the Irish problem. In the first place Redmond's association with the British war effort seriously weakened his authority – always on the side of moderation – over the Home Rule movement: the Volunteers split, with the extremist National Volunteers being formed under Professor McNeil. In the second place, Home Rule as promised by the Westminster Liberals, now to be delayed until the end of the war, began to seem a hollow sham: this appearance was strengthened with the formation of the first Coalition in which Unionist sentiment was strong.

Events moved dramatically from the arrest of Sir Roger Casement on April 22nd, 1916, to the Dublin Rising on Easter Monday, and the executions which followed. Asquith was now convinced that Home Rule must be enacted at once; apart from anything else heed must be paid to American sentiment in the matter. But there remained the problem of the Protestant minority concentrated in Ulster, originally a tactical move in the Unionist game, now grown into a real issue on its own account. The historic Ulster spread over nine counties, but a clear Protestant majority spread only to six. Lloyd George, the Government's prize negotiator, bargained with Ulstermen and Nationalists: there was no talk of partition; the six counties would simply be excluded from a settlement which would confer on the rest of Ireland the sort of arrangement obtaining today in the case of Northern Ireland. Negotiations broke down on the question of whether the exclusion was to be temporary or permanent.

In March, 1918, Redmond died. The proposal to extend conscription to Ireland (never implemented) brought a further accession of strength to Sinn Fein, now quite clearly the majority party. Seventy-eight Sinn Feiners were elected in the December election: they all refused to take their seats at Westminster.

After the election Lloyd George, for the first time, suggested partition, with a separate parliament in the north as well as the south. This was supposed to be a concession to the Nationalists since it was quite opposed to what the Ulstermen themselves wanted, and was designed to open the way to eventual 'coalescence'. It was unacceptable to the Nationalists committed to the ideal of a united Ireland, and now the accumulated bitterness of repeated delay, exacerbated by the ascendancy of Sinn Fein extremism, burst forth in guerilla warfare. After a succession of resignations the Government appointed as Irish Secretary a tough-skinned Canadian adventurer, Sir Hamer Greenwood. Only the continued sway of extreme Unionist sentiment – represented by Carson, Sir Henry Wilson, and Bonar Law – over the Cabinet, combined with the old refusal of the Briton to look at what was going on on his own doorstep, can explain the next developments. A policy of reprisals was inaugurated, backed by an army of occupation of 60,000, and carried through by an irregular force of roughnecks dredged from English slums, and out-of-work officers, out of place in a post-war world, recruited to reinforce the Royal Irish Constabulary. Under the notorious sobriquet of 'black and tans', this auxiliary force brought execration upon Britain's name.

Reprisal and counter-reprisal, arson and atrocity continued, to the growing disquiet of British opinion, until late 1921. On 6th December Lloyd George concluded the Treaty establishing the Irish Free State. It still embodied the partition actually enacted in 1920, but the Nationalists had made two gains: the Free State was to have Dominion status, and there was to be a boundary commission to delimit Ulster. However, the Irish question was far from settled: partition pleased no one. In the south, in particular, Irishmen now turned the fury lately directed against the black and tans against each other.

CHAPTER FOUR

RECESSION AND THE SIDEWAYS SHUFFLE IN SOCIAL REFORM

THE post-war boom reached its peak in the Spring of 1920 with a lunatic burst of speculation. The subsequent crash heralded the long cycle of depression which lasted until the Second World War. Since, however, there was a temporary recovery in 1923–4 when the French occupation of the Ruhr brought a cessation of German coal exports, and since modest economic progress was made from 1924 to 1929, the realities of the situation were to some extent concealed. Furthermore, the worst of the unemployment was confined to certain localized depressed areas, all far from London. Thus it was that while criticism of the economic mismanagement of the country heightened the general post-war scepticism, the reasonably well-off were still able to enjoy the gay irresponsibility engendered by this scepticism. Here we have the key to one aspect of life in the twenties.

In September, 1929, the collapse of the American stock market opened the way to an intensification of Britain's economic problems. Conditions did not in fact become desperate until the Spring of 1931: they then became so closely intertwined with the political situation that they must be considered separately under that heading. The point to be made here is that the crisis of 1931 was in reality an intensification of a slump which had been a continuous feature of the economy since 1920.

The most obvious characteristic of the slump was the high level of unemployment: by March, 1921, it had reached 1½ million or 10 per cent of the working population and it remained at this figure all through the twenties, till the crisis brought it up to almost 3 million. Unemployment was particularly concentrated in Lancashire, Tyneside, Cumberland, Scotland, and South Wales, where it often hovered around 50 per cent or more.

The dominant factor in this unhappy state of affairs was the collapse of the basic British export trades, discussed in Chapter Two. The post-war position in the coal industry was that while world production was expanding, demand, due in part to a general switch-over from coal to oil as fuel for the world's shipping, was shrinking. At home, too, the development of electricity, and the increased efficiency of gas production lessened demand. Employment in all industries was affected by increasing mechanization. Throughout the period, then, the coal, shipbuilding, iron and steel, and cotton industries were continuously in the doldrums, and the areas traditionally associated with them were 'depressed areas'.

The development of new industries, electricity, plastics, motor-cars, patent foods, 'luxuries', which, with only 6.5 per cent of Britain's total industrial output in 1907, reached 12.5 per cent in 1924, and 16.3 per cent in 1928, might have been expected to take up the slack. But the fact was that this expansion simply was not big enough. The new industries were established in the pleasant surroundings of the Home Counties, so that the problems of the depressed areas were not really touched. What was needed was a great programme of private or public investment in new industrial enterprises.

Not only did Government policy do nothing to encourage such investment: with single-minded intensity it actively discouraged it. The Cunliffe Committee recommended the orthodox return to deflation and dear money: in April, 1920, the Bank Rate was raised to 7 per cent, and there was a severe reduction in the Fiduciary Issue. Together these measures involved a drastic restriction in the credit which is essential to industrial expansion: the premium was on saving, not investment. Driven by a legion of terrified business men, the Lloyd George Government, in August, 1921, set up an Economy Committee under Sir Eric Geddes. At the beginning of the following year the 'Geddes Axe' chopped away a substantial section of public expenditure. The reduction of both public and private expenditure involved, naturally, a reduction in the community's total spending power, and therefore a reduction in the demand for the goods which British industry was already having difficulty enough in selling. Factors far beyond Government control had begun the vicious movement: Government policy turned it into a circle.

Financial orthodoxy was responsible for one other very serious error. In 1925 Churchill as Chancellor of the Exchequer was prevailed upon to return the country to the Gold Standard at the pre-war parity of pound to dollar, regardless of the fact that the pound had meantime dropped in value by at least 10 per cent. British industry was thus presented with the further handicap that foreigners were now expected to pay 10 per cent more for its exports (4·25 dollars for every pound's worth, instead of 3·85 dollars). Many industrialists felt that the only way out was to reduce costs by wage cuts equivalent to the 10 per cent, with momentous consequences as we shall see.

In general, then, this period marks a retreat on the part of the State from the commanding heights of the economy controlled during the war. Yet the progress of collectivism was not entirely interrupted: in 1926 the Baldwin Government was responsible for the setting up of both the British Broadcasting Corporation and the Central Electricity Board. What is more, the unprecedented unemployment level forced the State into greater activity in another direction. The original Lloyd George Unemployment Insurance Act of 1911 had been limited to 3 million participants among the lower paid workers: a new Insurance Act of November, 1920, increased this figure by a further 8 millions. But the whole system was designed to deal with the purely temporary spells of unemployment of pre-war days, and was ill-adapted to the needs of a community continuously unable to find work for one tenth of its employable population. In 1922 the rather nasty distinction was drawn between 'covenanted benefit', to which the worker was held to be entitled, and 'uncovenanted benefit', the dole, granted as an act of grace by the State, with a 'gap' during which the unemployed man was forced back on the assistance of the old Poor Law.

This nineteenth-century relic, however, was all but destroyed by the 1929 Local Government Act which transferred all the powers of the Poor Law Guardians to the County Councils. A triumph for the Minister of Health, Neville Chamberlain, and for rationalization, if not socialization, this giant Act cut through much of the confusion which had accumulated around local government since 1888, and gave the local authorities new powers over roads, town and country planning, public health, and maternity and child welfare. On the question of unemployment insurance itself, the State, by 1929, had assumed in the interests of its weakest members a burden of staggering proportions; yet administration was harsh, and payments (fifteen shillings a week for an adult male) niggardly. Unemployment in its two aspects, causation and palliation, remained the fundamental issue bringing governments of all complexions into bitter contempt.

While Government control of industry was relaxed, there was a resumption of industrial combination on a private basis. There had been giants in the late nineteenth century, but the first modern colossus was created in 1926 when Sir Alfred Mond and Sir Harry McGowan brought about the merger of Brunner, Mond, United Alkali, British Dyestuffs and Nobel Industries into Imperial Chemical Industries, with a total capital of £56 millions. In the new industrial pattern of vast public companies there was greater scope than ever before for the 'manager', often a scientist by training, who could wield an influence which bore no relation to any share capital which he might hold. The rise of the 'managerial class' was an important feature of twentieth century British society.

Orthodox economic theory was firmly in the saddle; it brooked neither halter nor bridle, but gave free rein to the economy. The one powerful attempt to unseat it came from a former treasury official, J. M. Keynes, who first hit public attention with his book, *The Economic Consequences of the Peace*. In concluding this work he remarked:

The true voice of the new generation has not yet spoken, and silent opinion is not yet formed. To the formation of the general opinion of the future I dedicate this work.

Keynes was to play Adam Smith to the Pitts and Huskissons of the post-1940 generation, but for the time being his influence on domestic economic policy was negligible, despite his *The Economic Consequences of Mr Churchill* (1925), and various pamphlets on credit and exchange control. Keynes did gain the ear of the Lloyd George section of the Liberal party, and the Liberal Yellow Book of 1928 was the one substantial political tract of the decade to show an understanding of the country's economic ailments. It may on the other hand be noted that in 1931 the Liberals emerged as the foremost enthusiasts for Government economy, a policy subsequently characterized by Keynes as 'replete with folly'.

As an avowedly anti-capitalist party, Labour might have been expected to have evolved a workable economic policy of its own: it hadn't. The progressive elements of the I.L.P., led by Clifford Allen, did, however, endeavour to hammer out an economic programme. The result was *The Living Wage* (1926) – written mainly by the economist, J. A. Hobson, and the socialist intellectual, H. N. Brailsford – which advocated nationalization of the Bank of England and of the basic industries, family allowances (as a means, in particular, of dealing with 'under-consumption'), and bulk purchase of imports.

In the first years of peace, the Labour movement tended to seek its ends through direct industrial action. The Russian Revolutions of 1917–18, naturally, had a profound influence, though even after a number of Marxist groups had coalesced in 1920 into the British Communist Party, that body had little influence on the working class as a whole. In fact the roots of the militance of 1919–22 lay elsewhere: particularly in the collapse of the war boom and the parallel collapse of Government promises, and in the weaknesses of Labour's parliamentary leadership. The troubles started at the beginning of 1919 with pitched battles in Glasgow between strikers and police, and spread to all areas and industries, finally settling in the coal industry, the chronic trouble spot of the twenties. The miners' struggles have become part of the literary lore of the twentieth century, *How Green Was My Valley* (1940) being perhaps the most successful novel to draw upon them.

State control of the mines ended on 31st March, 1921. At once the private owners imposed cuts unacceptable to the miners, who appealed for support to the Railwaymen and the Transport Workers, their partners in the pre-war trade union 'Triple Alliance'. Joint action, however, collapsed on 15th April – 'Black Friday', in labour history – and the miners fought on alone throughout the Summer. General militance subsided with the increased political activity of the Autumn of 1922 when the Labour party had some striking electoral successes. Even in 1925, when a Labour Government had come and gone, Stanley Baldwin was praying for 'peace in our time' in industry, and seemed to mean it.

The blow which shattered this tranquillity, and unleashed the chain of events leading to the country's only General Strike, was the restoration of the Gold Standard. Within two months the coal owners announced their intention of imposing longer hours and smaller wages. Led by Herbert Smith and A. J. Cook, the miners refused to discuss terms: this time they gained the united backing of the trade union movement, 31st July, 1925, becoming known as 'Red Friday'. In face of this threat of united action the Baldwin Government agreed to subsidize the industry until 1st May, 1926; yet another Royal Commission was appointed, this time under Sir Herbert Samuel. Why did the Government give in? Baldwin, with the 'appalling frankness' in which he gloried, later gave the answer: 'We weren't ready,' he explained.

The Government now set about making itself 'ready' for the next crisis. It gave its blessing to the privately sponsored Organization for the Maintenance of Supplies: if not as sinister as left-wing people maintained, this endorsement of any roughneck or rugger blue who cared to prepare himself for a spot of strike-breaking was scarcely a piece of high statesmanship. More important, a leading civil servant, Sir John Anderson, was set to the task of organizing the country to meet the emergency of a general strike. Having made its preparations the Government sat back to allow the owners and the miners to fight it out: it would have done better to direct its energies towards solving the basic problems of this depressed industry bedevilled by deplorable industrial relations.

On the trade union side there were no preparations, for the General Council of the TUC hoped that the report of the Samuel Commission would provide the basis for a settlement. The Samuel Report of 10th March, 1926, recommended reorganization of the industry just short of nationalization, but though, in principle, against wage reductions, it felt some immediate temporary cuts to be necessary. The Government ignored it: the miners deplored it; only the TUC General Council had any faith in the Report. This is the divergence which brought about the collapse of the General Strike.

On Saturday, 1st May, all the miners, refusing the terms imposed by the owners upon the termination of the Government subsidy, were out. Their slogan, coined by A. J. Cook with all the laborious attention he devoted to such matters, was 'Not a penny off the pay, not a minute on the day'. The executive committees of the various other unions, previously committed to the support of the miners, now met, and agreed to hand all powers over to the General Council. This was the first real preparation for a general strike made by the union – two days before it began. Did this decision simply mean that the General Council now had powers to negotiate on behalf of the miners, or did it mean that the General Council had to fight things out until a settlement satisfactory to the miners was reached? The miners believed the latter: the General Council the former. It is an extension of the divergence we noted above.

Satisfied that everything was in train for a general strike the miners' representatives left London. This involved a delay when the General Council wanted to consult the miners in regard to the negotiations which it was still conducting with the Government; this delay annoyed the Cabinet, and probably hardened its determination. However, discussions between the Cabinet and the negotiating committee of the General Council continued late on the night of Sunday, 2nd May, when news came through that the *Daily Mail* printers had refused to allow the Monday edition to go to press because they objected to its leading article on the strike situation. On this flimsy pretext the Government, increasingly under pressure from its right-wingers, broke off negotiations. In this sense it was finally responsible for precipitating the General Strike which began at midnight on 3rd May.

Within its limits the strike was highly successful, and no substantial return to work took place before it was called off: it was clear that throughout the working class there was genuine support for the miners. There was no plan, but rather, under the inspiration of Ernest Bevin, a great feat of improvisation. In reply to Winston Churchill's *British Gazette* the unions printed a *British Worker*. The General Council insisted that this was an industrial, not a political strike, and firmly excluded over-eager leftist politicians from the central direction.

The hope of the trade unions was that the strike would produce such chaos that the Government would be forced to negotiate. In fact in the fine May weather the ordinary life of the community continued to tick over: the Government had the use of the BBC: and the general public, though sympathetic towards the miners, felt that this challenge to the constitution must be resisted. On the other side, trade union funds could not hold out for ever, nor could the risk that a violent clash might bring about the total destruction of the trade union movement be ignored.

Thus the counsels of the moderate trade union leaders Thomas and Pugh began to gain sway. What the General Council wanted was a middle man to conduct negotiations without loss of face: this they found in Samuel, who independently and unofficially put forward the Samuel Memorandum which suggested a settlement along the lines of his own Royal Commission. The Memorandum was not accepted by the Government, though mainly through the petty dishonesty of Baldwin and of Thomas the General Council allowed itself to believe that it was, and with indecent haste brought the strike to an end at noon on 12th May. The miners had not been consulted: no terms had been secured. Twenty-four hours later, the individual unions, disgusted with their leaders, had brought 100,000 more men out. But the vital unity was shattered: the miners fought on alone, till the winter and starvation drove them back.

The collapse of the General Strike put a final period to the post-war militancy of the British trade unions. It brought disillusionment and a drastic drop in membership, which in 1927 fell below 5 millions for the first time since 1916. The Trade Union Act of 1927 declared general strikes illegal, and altered the basis of the trade union contribution to the finances of the Labour party: the individual trade unionist now had to 'contract in' to payment of the political levy instead of 'contracting out' if he did not want to pay it. Apathy was no longer on the side of the angels, and Labour party funds naturally dropped.

Industrial relations in the late twenties became pervaded by the ideas of co-operation and 'peace in industry' associated with the industrialist, Sir Alfred Mond, and the T U C leader, Ben Turner. A second, and more vigorous, step was decided upon by Ernest Bevin, who was now clearly emerging as the greatest trade union leader of his generation: Bevin decided that instead of undertaking independent, and futile, industrial action, the T U C must exert a more direct influence on the Labour party.

Despite the depression and the defeats, which meant that about one tenth of the entire working population was earning less than the bare minimum needed to support a family, the British working man had not entirely lost the gains of the war period. Wages had almost doubled their pre-war level to average three pounds per week, and hours had dropped from an average of about fifty-five per week to about forty-eight per week (A. L. Bowley, *Wages and Income since 1860*). Although prices had kept up with wages the important point was that there still remained a greatly increased *margin* for 'luxuries' or for setting against hard times.

It was this margin, combined with another economic innovation which spread rapidly in the twenties (it had actually been pioneered in this country by the Singer Sewing Machine Company in Victorian times), Hire Purchase, which created another social trend which is only showing its full consequences in our own time. In the twenties and thirties the working man still had little enough stake in the community; but in the fifties and sixties he was to be almost as deeply financially committed through his hire purchase borrowings, as the middle class had always been. He then (or his wife did) began to show, among other things, a traditionally middle-class reluctance to resort to strike action.

CHAPTER FIVE

THE GAY TWENTIES

INNOVATION, freedom, and scepticism were the character-istics of British society in the twenties. We have already examined the roots of the scepticism, and the irresponsible gaiety which accompanied it. We are not here thinking simply of the wealthier classes: social history is not the history of high society. Much of the working class, as we have seen, was materially much better off than ever before; life in many ways was becoming easier.

However, the intellectual attitudes which help to form the ethos of any particular age almost always percolate down from above. Neither of the two prophets of the age, Sigmund Freud and Albert Einstein, was British. It was not till the twenties that the theories of Freud, due in part to the impassioned discipleship of Ernest Jones, gained wide currency in Britain. They were not always strictly interpreted. Popularly conceived, the theories of the libido and the subconscious encouraged free experiment in the expression of natural instincts, and brought a final challenge to Victorian moral restraints. Einstein's Theory of Relativity could be seen as a challenge not only to Newtonian physics, but to all accepted absolutes. 'Every-thing,' as John Galsworthy expressed it in the preface to his *Modern Comedy*, a trilogy of novels covering the early twenties,

being now relative, there is no longer absolute dependence to be placed on God, Free Trade, Marriage, Consols, Coal or Caste.

Relativity and the Quantum Theory involve what would seem, to the logical mind, to be contradictions and absurdities. In the new view of the universe, common sense and logic were no longer enough; the emphasis would now be on the sub-jective and irrational.

British figures of importance were Havelock Ellis, whose *Studies in the Psychology of Sex* had been published before the war, and Dr Marie Stopes, author of *Married Love* and propagandist of contraception. To the concepts of Einstein there was greater resistance among British scientists. A continental physicist had once remarked to Rutherford that Anglo-Saxons could not understand Relativity; 'no, they've got too much sense,' was Rutherford's rejoinder. In fact, despite its great practical achievements British physics showed great limitations in the theoretical and philosophical side. In 1927 Arthur Eddington, mathematician and astronomer, published his *Stars and Atoms*, which was the prelude to a number of other works of general exposition; the success of these books illustrates the general enthusiasm for, and interest in, science. It was with the avowed intention of going one better than Eddington that James Jeans, who had himself turned from atomic physics to astronomy, produced in 1930 his *Mysterious Universe*. Beautifully written, this is very much a product of the age in its attempt to reconcile the new science with, what people still wanted to believe in, the existence of an Absolute. Thus (p. 134):

from the intrinsic evidence of his creation, the Great Architect of the Universe now begins to appear as a pure mathematician.

In his middle of the road, comfortable, compromising manner, Sir James Jeans was the Stanley Baldwin of science.

Bertrand Russell (born 1872) was both a 'pure' philosopher of the highest distinction, and a barometer of social change. For his activities with the No Conscription Fellowship during the war he had been imprisoned and had been deprived of his Cambridge Fellowship. He published a very critical study of Bolshevism in 1920, and in the later years of the decade ran one of the many progressive schools which were a feature of the period. Hand in hand with advanced educational notions went advanced nutritional nostrums. There was something of a fetish for vitamins in the twenties, thanks largely to the discoveries of Frederick Gowland Hopkins (who at last, in 1924, was given an Institute of Biochemistry at Cambridge).

The new intellectual attitudes found their most direct expression in the arts, for this decade, despite all the other criticisms that can be made of it, was one of the most vital in British cultural history. Perhaps the war, in setting a period to British political and commercial supremacy, had also released the wells of artistic sensibility. The twenties, at least, did not have the preoccupation with material gain, with thrift, and with social status, which so often marred the work of the Victorians. For the English novel, this was an age of brilliance *Liter.* (the sun, of course, shone on both sides of the Atlantic, on Hemingway and Fitzgerald, as well as on Huxley, Joyce, Lawrence, Virginia Woolf, and E. M. Forster).

The Aldous Huxley of the twenties is the quick-witted critic of the upper crust society of his times. He shows little concern with, or knowledge of, the less glittering segments of society. The much more popular Galsworthy, likewise, was concerned solely, as he admitted, with the 10 per cent 'above the property line'. Huxley's later work takes on a much more profound hue: *Brave New World* (1931) is perhaps the turning-point – it is a vision of the future, seen very definitely from the twenties, by a man with an understanding of the fullest implications of the new biological sciences. With his two last great novels, *Ulysses* and *Finnegans Wake*, James Joyce brought technical innovation in the novel practically to breaking-point. They stand exactly at the opposite pole to *The Mysterious Universe*: the intellectual life of the decade is represented by the crackling magnetic field in between.

Disillusionment is the keynote of the verse of T. S. Eliot at this time (like Huxley he changes with the new decade): in the *Waste Land* is to be found desolation at its most desolate. Disgust with the war showed itself strongly in a number of more ephemeral books and plays. The *avant-garde* dramatist, curious as it may seem now, was Noël Coward, who in a fruitful partnership with C. B. Cochran, the impresario, launched a number of biting revues.

A lot of British painting wore its debt to the recent French *Art.* masters too openly upon its sleeve. But there could be no gainsaying the creative independence of Augustus John, who continued to add to his pre-war reputation. Younger men like Matthew Smith, Edward Wadsworth and Duncan Grant established themselves for the first time. Ben Nicholson was the artist who, flitting enthusiastically from one coterie to another, best expressed in his life and work the sense of innovation and the nihilism of the period. But despite the enthusiastic championship of the critics, Roger Fry and Clive Bell, popular taste still lagged well behind the latest developments. The modernistically conceived posters of E. McKnight Kauffer, which decorated the London Underground, met with general acceptance, but the sculpture of Epstein, particularly his 'Rima', aroused popular outcry. Thus began the vicious circle which has left permanent scars. Unappreciated by the masses, the artists and intellectuals of the period developed an untoward arrogance which detached them still further from society as a whole.

Music With the twentieth century there has come an astounding renaissance in British music. It is particularly difficult for the historian to explain why this should be so, since music is the purest of all art forms, the one least related to social or representational elements. Certainly the herald of the new dawn, Edward Elgar, was a man of his age: in the overture, 'Cockaigne', and in the 'Pomp and Circumstance' marches are to be found all the Edwardian extravagance of capitalism's last summer; and the 'Cello Concerto of 1919 is the concentrated longing of a man looking back upon a world which has gone for ever. But the music of Vaughan Williams and Arnold Bax cannot easily be related to the intellectual climates of the twenties we have been discussing. Vaughan Williams looked back to Tudor polyphony and English folk music, and Bax to the Celtic renaissance of the 1890's. There was a more specifically twentyish quality about the music of William Walton, which at times incorporated jazz rhythms. It might not unfairly be said that the British music of this time was modern, but not too modern. The composer thus retained his individual integrity, and an audience: the audience was not big, but it slowly increased; this was the basis upon which the revival of British music continued.

Architecture stands at the opposite end of the scale to music: it is the art form most obviously related to contemporary social trends. The Government in 1920 stood pledged to build 'homes fit for heroes', but a decent rate of building was only achieved between 1924 and 1927 when the Wheatley Act, which involved intensified State action in this sphere, was in force. Thanks to the work of Howard and Unwin in the first decade of the century, the rudiments of planning had been relearned; and British domestic architecture, under the influence of Voysey, had been the study and admiration of foreigners. Such houses as were built were reasonably well designed and situated in fairly well planned estates, laid out, however, according to a rigid class segregation. Ribbon development along the main highways was open to criticism on even broader grounds, and the many mannerisms of the domestic builder were to find an effective satirist in Osbert Lancaster: this was the age of 'Stockbrokers' Tudor' and 'Bypass Variegated'. The greatest venture was Britain's second garden city, begun in 1920 at Welwyn. The theories of the Swiss architect Le Corbusier did not become current in Britain till 1927: British public architecture then for a time suffered from the absurd, one might say irresponsible, application of his 'gospel of function'.

Religion

The various intellectual and artistic influences we have been discussing all served to assist the decline in religion set decisively in train by the disruptions of the war (though we have noted the pre-war attitude of Ann Veronica). Parallel with the absolute decline in church-going in all the non-Catholic denominations went clear gains on the part of the authoritarian and ritualistic persuasions – the Catholics and, to a lesser extent, the Anglo Catholics. This may be seen as a function of the re-enthronement of the irrational, or as an extension of the concept of relativity: if one standpoint is as good as another, why not the total standpoint of the Church of Rome? The progress of Catholicism was represented, and furthered, by a number of prominent literary converts, including Hilaire Belloc, G. K. Chesterton and Compton Mackenzie. For parliament, the growth of Anglo Catholicism provoked the

1927 Prayer Book controversy; by an irony implicit in the position of an Established Church, a non-Anglican majority in the House of Commons secured the rejection of the new Prayer Book. Finally, the 1920's saw a Mormon invasion, and the inception of what was later to be known as Moral Rearmament; for the time being, to the dismay of the ancient seat of learning, it was content to call itself the Oxford Group.

Religion was decreasingly affecting the life of the people of Britain; what did have a profound effect was the general easing of the burdens of life, despite the prevailing economic depression. To take two random but significant examples: the Edwardian custard was a thing of eggs, sugar, milk, and mixing and beating, and, therefore, time: the appearance of ready-made custard powders in the 1920's turned a heavy ritual into a mere formality; similarly the introduction of stainless steel cutlery meant that the old daily immolation of time, polish, and elbow-grease could be replaced by an occasional lip service. More important – and it is upon this ground, perhaps, more than any other, that the First World War stands as a vital turning-point in British social history – was the apparent disappearance, with the advances in health and hygiene and in State services generally, of the old 'submerged tenth', the 'dirty poor'. No longer was it a good joke to believe that if you gave the poor a bath they would simply put their coal in it: all houses built after the war contained bathrooms. Certainly there was a new depressed class in the unemployed of the heavy industrial areas: but these were a different race, men of spirit and self-respect, who would not remain permanently submerged.

In fine, class distinctions were blurred, though not, of course, obliterated: with the war had come a new fluidity in social groupings, different altogether from Edwardian times when great wealth had simply represented a one-way ticket to the top. All the same it must be admitted that Britain remained basically a class society, though the distinctions and differences were now infinitely subtle. The general level of dress improved and became standardized: still there were at the top these explicit, and sometimes exciting, changes known as fashion. For woman the chief aim was to look as little like a woman as possible, doubtless, in part, a confused response to the political emancipation of 1918: hence the fetching boyish lines of the twenties. For man, for whom changes in fashion are well-nigh irreversible, the landmark was the appearance in 1924 of 'Oxford Bags'. The long-term effect was general widening of trouser bottoms; this has lasted to the present day save for those men who are in the height of the new slim-line fashion, and those older men who have never changed.

British education was not greatly improved in the 1920's. The promise of the Fisher Act was stifled in the Lloyd George economy campaign: the rather tentative suggestions of the Hadow Report of 1926 were similarly smothered in 1931 before they ever came into force. The private preparatory schools and the great Public Schools, catering for about six per cent of the population, remained as slender but strong pillars of the caste system. In the first post-war flush the Headmasters' Conference had indeed proposed to offer a Public School education to all ex-elementary boys who could profit by it; but no machinery was set up to implement this proposal. In a notorious speech at Harrow, Baldwin, with his tongue perhaps not wholly lodged in his cheek, remarked: 'When the call came for me to form a Government, one of my first thoughts was that it should be a Government of which Harrow should not be ashamed. I remembered how in previous Governments there had been four, or perhaps five, Harrovians, and I determined to have six.'

The post-war tide of change did indeed reach as far as the ancient English Universities, washing away compulsory Greek, and throwing up new courses in the sciences and in economics and politics. In addition to the four ancient Scottish Universities, there were by 1926 also universities at London, Durham, Manchester, Liverpool, Birmingham, Leeds, Sheffield, Bristol, and Reading, and university colleges at Nottingham, Southampton, Exeter, Hull, and Leicester. The University Grants Committee had been set up in 1911, and in 1920 came the institution of state scholarships. All in all, the student population of England and Wales increased from 12,778 in 1909–10 to 40,465 in 1935–36 – still not a very striking figure. An inadequate elementary education continued to be the lot of most.

There was, however, a tremendous expansion in mass communication in the 1920's. The British Broadcasting Company of 1922, financed in the first instance by the wireless manufacturers, became a Public Corporation in 1926, a state monopoly based on the revenue derived from individual licence holders of whom there were over two million by the end of the year. The presiding eminence of the new BBC was John (later Lord) Reith, who gave British broadcasting its distinctive flavouring of presbyterian unctuousness and spinsterish caution. None the less, the new institution was firmly established by the end of the decade, its artistic standards were, on the whole, high, and its educatory motives laudable. Much of the criticism directed against the BBC, in fact, was grossly unfair.

The BBC was perhaps rather slow in recognizing the potential of the experiments in television of John Logie Baird. Baird, for various reasons, is a figure worthy of some attention. In his utter difference from the Cambridge scientists we have described he almost suggests a throw-back to the workshop or garret inventors and innovators of the early industrial revolution. On the other hand, in his attempts to found an industry based on his discoveries he was very much of the twentieth century. Above all, the new medium which Baird pioneered is perhaps the strongest single influence in British society today.

Born in 1888, Baird was the son of a Helensburgh minister. (The importance of Scottish Calvinism in British science and technology is a persistent theme since the eighteenth century.) After various commercial exploits, including the promotion of 'The Baird Undersock' and the manufacture of jam in the Caribbean (the stock eventually being knocked down to a London merchant for use in the manufacture of sausages), he devoted himself in the twenties to the problems of the transmission of pictures by wireless, a question then much discussed, though generally discounted by the knowledgeable.

Baird exploited crucial discoveries of others; similar experiments to his were made almost simultaneously in America; he long failed to appreciate the value of the cathode ray tube and of short-wave transmission; but having said all that, it was still Baird who in 1925 achieved the first transmission of a recognizable image.

Despite a series of public demonstrations thereafter, the BBC remained lukewarm. By 1934 when it had decided definitely upon the importance of this branch of broadcasting, the Marconi-EMI combine had developed an efficient rival British system and it was this, almost to Baird's heartbreak, that was finally adopted. It may be noted here that television as a feature of national life was still in its swaddling clothes when the 1939 war put it into a long slumber. During this war Baird successfully experimented with colour television, but before the fruits could be gathered his physique, never robust, finally gave out in 1945.

Meanwhile a final revolution was taking place in the newspaper world. The resort to display advertising on the part of the great departmental stores completed the process whereby journalism became big business dependent for survival upon the maintenance of huge circulations. Three great newspaper empires were consolidated in the 1920's: those of Lord Rothermere, Lord Beaverbrook, and the Berry brothers. With Beaverbrook's *Express* now challenging the *Daily Mail* for the leadership of the popular press, the rivalry between these two set the pattern for the cut-throat newspaper competition which broke out in the last years of the decade. Of all the various consequences of the new newspaper imperialism, perhaps the unhappiest for the community as a whole was the decimation of the provincial Press, repository of much that had been finest in nineteenth-century British journalism.

Since its foundation in 1911 by George Lansbury, the *Daily Herald* had been the cinderella of the British Press. Though taken over by the TUC in 1922 it still had the greatest difficulty in making ends meet. It was the conjunction in 1929 of Ernest Bevin and J. S. Elias, the presiding genius of the sensationalist Odhams Press, which brought about the launching of a new *Daily Herald*, with a one-million circulation, on 17th March, 1930. The field was set for the intensified circulation war of the early thirties.

It is not surprising after all this to find that the general leisure pursuits of the people fell rather short of the intellectual activities mentioned at the beginning of the chapter. Indeed there was yet another form of mass communication which expanded hugely in the early twenties: this was the cinema. It soon became apparent that Britain was curiously lacking in the kind of talent needed to exploit the new medium, so that from 1922 America was able to establish a stranglehold on the British market. By insisting on the bulk export of film, Hollywood unleashed a flood of the third-rate and trivial, all but obscuring the occasional masterpiece of the cinematic art. The great heroes of this age were Rudolph Valentino, Tom Mix, Douglas Fairbanks, Gloria Swanson, and, of course, Charlie Chaplin, whose films can be taken as expressing the finest aspect of the gaiety of the twenties – man's brave laughter in face of a cruel and crazy world.

The growth of broadcasting was partly responsible for a slump which hit the British cinema trade in 1926–7. The advent of 'Talkies' from 1926, and the building of luxury cinemas of the type familiar to us today, made, however, for a fairly rapid recovery; by 1939 weekly attendances had reached 19 millions. The British Cinematograph Films Act of 1927 is a sign both of the stirrings of collectivist concern in the matter of mass entertainment, and of alarm over the American stranglehold. The Act established a quota system, and set up a Committee to advise the Board of Trade on matters concerning the film industry. A considerable boost was thus given to British film-making, though the fruits did not really begin to become apparent till the thirties.

This was not a heroic decade, for all the dynamic experimentation. It was a golden age of dancing: the frenzied Vampire and Shimmy cooled off into the Blues of 1923, then 1924 boiled up again in the Charleston of the following year. The twenties, too, provide abundant material to illustrate the British penchant for succumbing to absurd crazes. In late

1921 film stars and society figures raced each other on a type of stilt on springs – the pogo stick. 'From Pogo Stick to Bingo Boom' – that would be a perfect title for a study of British life and leisure since the twenties, sociologically very revealing since while pogo sticks were really the prerogative of the upper set, bingo is the pastime of all classes.

For the first time a clearly marked 'mass culture', based on growing standardization and commercialization and increased American influence, had begun to appear, thus throwing the countervalent 'minority culture' into sharp relief. It was a division which the leading artistic and intellectual figures, in their exclusiveness and disdain for the public as a whole, did much to foster. The growth of social welfare was not, in itself, solving all the problems of human society.

CHAPTER SIX

OUTWARD APPEARANCES

FOREIGN policy is, up to a point, the outward projection of a country's economic interests and social ideologies. In the upheavals of the First World War the other side of the equation became equally true for Britain: economic conditions and social attitudes were themselves conditioned by the flow of world events over which Britain had little or no control. Although Britain had defeated her greatest continental rival, in the struggle the last elements of a true world supremacy had vanished: her relatively unscathed ally, the United States, had now attained, if she cared to assert it, at least equal status in the counsels of the nations. International relations, then, are to be considered here both as a product of the forces we have already discussed, and as a powerful force operating in its own right upon British society. Above all we must pick out the train of events which, at the end of the next decade, plunged British society again into the melting-pot of a world war.

While the advance of collectivism has had its counterpart in the growth of the ideas of international co-operation and collective security embodied in such institutions as the League of Nations and the United Nations, British external policy since 1914 does not at first sight completely fit the pattern of this book. For one thing it is always much more difficult to put idealism into practice in foreign policy than in domestic policy. Furthermore there are always far stronger resistances to a progressive foreign policy: patriotism may be enlisted on the side of having the best health service in the world, but it may not agree to the submission of national interests to an international authority. In effect, two entirely contrary current opinions threw up the frothy confusion which was British foreign policy after 1918.

What may be called the forward movement was inspired by Labour and Liberal internationalists, and by a few idealistic aristocrats like Lord Robert Cecil and Lord Parmoor. It appeared to have some support from Lloyd George and some of the politicians, who, in face of the terrible slaughter at the Western Front, had evolved the justification that the war was being fought 'to end war', or 'to make the world safe for democracy'. Early in 1918, Lloyd George, as we have seen, had made a declaration of peace aims; he was then put in the position of having to accept President Wilson's Fourteen Points, which called, among other things, for a peace without indemnities, and a new world order based on the principles of democracy and nationalism.

The main aims of the forward movement were some form of international government – a League of Nations; a peace based on democracy and national self-determination; fair treatment of Germany; and an end to the old secret diplomacy, which was held to have been primarily responsible for the war. The strength of the forward movement can be seen from the support accorded throughout the inter-war years to the non-political body founded to publicize the ideals of the League of Nations – the League of Nations Union.

The backward movement, however, read the lessons of the war in a different way: the horrors had been so terrible that someone must be held accountable. Hence the cries of the less inhibited coalition supporters for 'hanging the Kaiser', and for squeezing Germany 'till the pips squeak'. Such policies had strong support from inflamed British public opinion. In sections of the Conservative party where foreign policy and diplomacy had long been regarded as the prerogative of an *élite* there was no loss of faith in the old diplomacy, and no real trust in the idea of a League of Nations. The adherents of the backward movement, Balfour, Curzon, and Austen Chamberlain, were in office for almost ten years; the forward men, MacDonald and Henderson, for just over two. The first years of peace were, in fact, dominated by Lloyd George, now hoist with his chameleon petard.

We must glance back to the Peace Conference, which opened at Versailles in January, 1919. The main settlement with Germany was not signed till the end of June: meanwhile Germans continued to starve behind the Allied blockade. On the question of establishing Germany's frontiers a sharp disagreement between Britain and France quickly emerged. France was less concerned to make the world safe for democracy than to make the world safe for France: after two invasions at the hands of a neighbour who had almost twice her population, this was not surprising. Refused a Germany confined behind the Rhine, France had to be satisfied with a demilitarized German Rhineland, and a joint British and American guarantee against German aggression. This latter was exactly what France wanted; unfortunately the guarantee collapsed upon the failure of the United States' Senate to ratify the Versailles treaty, which provided an excuse for Britain, also, to withdraw.

Germany's eastern frontier likewise provoked disagreement. In accordance with the ideals of the forward movement, a national Polish state, submerged since the partitions of the eighteenth century, was created. So intermixed were the Poles and the Germans in some areas, that the drawing of boundaries on purely ethnological grounds presented the greatest difficulties. Clemenceau for France backed the Polish demands, meeting resistance from Lloyd George and Woodrow Wilson, who stood closer to the principles of pure self-determination. Finally the settlement in Upper Silesia was to be left to a plebiscite, Danzig was to be a free city, and there was to be a Polish corridor, giving Poland access to the sea, but cutting off East Prussia from the rest of Germany.

On the whole the territorial settlement as it affected Germany was a pretty fair one; the good intentions of President Wilson, and, to a lesser degree, of Lloyd George, who, in any event, could not wholly ignore the continued anti-German fervour of his own supporters and public opinion, were bound to be hampered by the *realpolitik* of Clemenceau and Orlando, who had, perforce, to point out that Italy had only entered the war for the sake of certain territorial gains. More open to criticism were the clauses which placed the 'War Guilt' on German shoulders, and their corollary, the exaction from Germany of Reparations. Indemnities from a defeated power were no new feature in history. France and Belgium clearly had a strong claim for reparation for the havoc wrought upon their own soil and in their most valuable industrial sectors. But a Reparations Agreement based on German responsibility for all the damage inflicted upon the Allies made a mockery of the latter's claim to be regarded as moderate and responsible peacemakers.

No total figure was fixed. How was it to be calculated? How was Germany to make payment anyway? There was only one way: by exports of coal and industrial manufactures. As far as Britain was concerned these would simply conflict with her own industries, themselves about to feel the full blast of post-war industrial depression. These criticisms were pungently expressed by J. M. Keynes in his *Economic Consequences of the Peace*. Indeed, Britain whose real need was a restoration of normal trading relations with the rest of the world, including Germany, again differed from France, whose prime concern was the reconstruction of her devastated territories. Britain would have done better to forswear reparations altogether for herself, insisting instead upon a real assistance to French reconstruction.

Two other aspects of the Peace Settlement were of lasting importance. A League of Nations, an embodiment of the century-old ideal of Lord Castlereagh interpreted in the light of the ideals of the new forward movement in foreign policy, was incorporated in the structure of the Versailles treaty itself. The League of Nations organized in a Council of the big powers plus an equal number of lesser ones, and a General Assembly of the small powers, was to have no sovereignty over its individual members. Its Covenant called upon members to resist aggression against fellow members by any means recommended by the Council. The League, then, would be exactly what the powers made of it: no more, no less. Initially both Germany and Russia were excluded. It may be noted that, at first, many members of the British Left were hostile, calling for a 'League of Peoples' instead of what they described as a 'League of Victorious Allies'.

In the Middle East the collapse of the Turkish Empire was met by the division of the Arab states into French and British mandates, along lines settled by the Sykes-Picot Agreement of 16th May, 1916. Of even greater significance for the future was the Balfour Declaration of 1917, guaranteeing the Jews a new national home in Palestine.

The first few years of peace were marked by a series of grandiose international conferences admirably adapted to Lloyd George's love of the limelight, which did little beyond revealing the increasing incompatibility of British and French attitudes towards foreign policy. The last and greatest failure was the Economic Conference which opened at Genoa in April, 1922, from which the Russians and Germans quietly took time off to conclude their own agreement at Rapallo. All too successful in their repudiation of secret diplomacy, these conferences, regrettably, completely by-passed the nascent League of Nations.

With the final destruction of the Turkish Empire only the Turks themselves had still to win their independence. Immediate success attended the nationalist revolution of 1920 led by Mustapha Kemal. In September, 1922, after a drive against the Greeks, who had been encroaching on Turkish territory, the Turks found themselves approaching the British lines at Chanak, near Troy. Hoping, apparently, to create a resurgence of jingoistic sentiment, or alternatively, it has been said, determined to resist aggression, Lloyd George threatened the Turks with the full might of the British Empire should they advance further. The Chanak incident passed over, but the surge of war-weary disapproval in Britain was sufficient to topple Lloyd George from office.

Lloyd George had practically ignored the existence of the League of Nations, in part, perhaps, because it had at the outset suffered a heavy blow in the withdrawal of the United States; in British Government circles there tended to be a feeling that the brunt of any action recommended by the League would inevitably fall on Britain, Europe's only great naval power. The League suffered its first open reverse over the Corfu incident of 1923, which is also important as Mussolini's first piece of international nose-thumbing. Briefly, in dealing with a rather minor dispute with Greece, Mussolini had taken the law into his hands to the extent of bombarding Corfu. He refused to accept League intervention, and had the matter instead referred to the Conference of Ambassadors, which represented the older diplomatic tradition. In acceding readily to this importunity the British Conservative Government had shown little concern for the prestige of the League.

This was in part remedied the following year when Labour's Ramsay MacDonald became the first Prime Minister actually to attend a meeting of the League. It also fell to the Labour Government to consider, and reject, Lord Robert Cecil's Draft Treaty of Mutual Assistance, designed to strengthen and speed up the security provisions of the Covenant. In its place MacDonald, along with the French Minister, Herriot, drew up the Geneva Protocol, which, although on similar lines, put greater emphasis on the possibilities for disarmament which greater security would create. But sections of the Labour movement still shied at the suggestion of any British military commitment, and it is far from clear that, even if it had remained in office, the Government would have been able to ratify the Protocol. As it was the Conservatives dropped the project.

The League reached its peak, in theory if not in practice, with the entry of Germany in 1925. But British foreign policy had already turned in another direction, towards, as the new Foreign Secretary, Austen Chamberlain, put it, 'knitting together the nations most nearly concerned, and whose differences might lead to a renewal of strife, by means of treaties framed with the sole object of maintaining, as between themselves, an unbroken peace'. A retreat in fact towards specific pacts, instead of the collective guarantees of the League, similar in kind to the retreat from collectivism in domestic policy. The most important product of the Chamberlain policy was the Locarno treaties of December, 1925, by which Britain and Italy guaranteed the existing Franco-German frontier.

The last years of the twenties were the years of pactomania, exemplified by the Kellogg-Briand pact which simply renounced war: an excellent sentiment, but of no greater force than the equally admirable sermon of the preacher who, without detailing precise remedies, was 'against sin'.

The twin aims of the statesmen of the period were security and disarmament. On the former topic the twenties ended in a blaze of rather ill-founded optimism. On the latter, progress was almost entirely confined to naval matters, still of great importance to a commercial nation like Britain. The Washington Naval Conference of 1921–22 established naval ratios by which Britain and America were to be as 5, to Japan's 3, to France and Italy's 1·6; the figures themselves express Britain's loss of her naval supremacy. At the London Naval Conference of 1930, the settlement was America and Britain as 10, to Japan's 7. France found herself unable to participate in this settlement.

Beside all this, the Reparations issue, so important at the time, must now be accounted rather academic. The problem was complicated by the large debts owed by the European countries to the United States. A general scaling-down and cancelling out of debts all round was suggested in the Balfour Note of August, 1922. This America, reasonably enough, and France, resisted, and ultimately Britain simply defaulted on her repayments to America. With the cessation of German payments in December, 1922, came the first big Reparations crisis: France, to strong British disapproval, invaded the Ruhr. The basic German grievance was still that no total figure had been settled; the Dawes Plan of 1924 was a great advance in that it settled a maximum annual figure; and finally the Young Plan of 1930 fixed the total amount. In the end Germany received more in loans than she paid out in Reparations, and with the financial crash of 1931 the whole undignified farce was wiped away.

Russia occupied a rather special position in the foreign policy of the period. Apart from anything else it provided a vital domestic political issue in a sense that other international topics did not. Bolshevik Russia from the start was the blackest bogeyman of the British upper and middle classes, which, in the first stages of the peace, found themselves committed to the White counter-revolutionaries in the civil strife still proceeding in Russia. Intervention actually had begun during the war as an attempt to bolster those elements in Russia still prepared to fight on against Germany. Some members of the Cabinet, of whom Churchill was one, wished to extend the British activities: Lloyd George, on the whole, was unfavourable. Crisis point at home was reached in May, 1920, when it was believed that the Government intended to assist the Poles in their war against the Soviet Union. Labour, still in the first flush of its post-war strength, protested strongly, and the Government, like a jaded Don Juan on the run, announced that its intentions had been misunderstood.

One of the first acts of the 1924 Labour Government was to grant *de jure* recognition to the Soviet régime. It tried to follow this up with a commercial treaty, but itself succumbed to the hostility this proposal aroused. The succeeding Conservative Government took an anti-Bolshevik line, as shown by its raid on the Russian trading company, Arcos, in May, 1927.

At the time, true to the domestic trends of the twenties, people felt a certain detached optimism about the developments in international politics. But just as in social reform this was a decade of lost opportunity, it must now stand out even more tragically as such in international relations. Particularly unfortunate was the failure of understanding between France and Britain. France could be indicted for her harshness towards Republican Germany; Britain for her failure to assuage French fears. But what counted most was the isolationism of the United States, for the great international consequence of the war was that America now occupied the important peripheral position which had once been Britain's.

C

CHAPTER SEVEN

THE POLITICS OF PYGMIES, 1922–31

TWENTIETH-century Britain has a certain importance in world history as a successful exponent of the form of government described as democracy, yet there is nothing specifically or necessarily democratic about the five cardinal features of the modern British Constitution: Crown, Cabinet, Prime Minister, Parliament, and Party. The relationships between these institutions were being worked out at a time when democracy was still regarded as a bad word, though it would be true to say that our modern parties are essentially a product of the widening of the electorate in the second half of the nineteenth century. It is through party that public opinion, widely diffused in a mass electorate, is drawn up and given concrete expression: 'Party', Disraeli said, 'is organized opinion'; the old Prime Minister in Maurice Edelman's *Who Goes Home?* describes it as 'organized conscience', and adds that though bad for the soul, this system is good for the nation. Democracy can be regarded as a sixth and final feature of the British Constitution which permeates and transforms the venerable five.

The form of British democracy is incorporated in universal suffrage, practically granted by the Act of 1918: the substance in freedom of speech, freedom of assembly, freedom from economic and social dependence, and a basic level of education. The advancement of freedom from economic and social dependence is but another way of describing the collectivist trends we have already discussed. The advancing powers of the state in themselves present a constitutional problem; clearly there is a danger that individual liberty may be diminished rather than increased. This is the central political problem of the democratic collectivist state.

Professor Mowat has characterized the politics of the period after the fall of Lloyd George as 'the rule of the pygmies' (*Britain between the Wars*, p. 142). There is truth in this. The giants were out: Lloyd George never returned to office, Winston Churchill spent long spells in the wilderness. Was it that there was now a strange dearth of political talent? Or was it that the 'gay twenties' demanded self-effacement and moderate courses from its politicians? This, after all, was the first decade of the new collectivist democracy, *free from the sanctions of war*: a difficult time for a would-be Gladstone or Disraeli. Perhaps we have been unduly influenced by Churchill's pungent comments on his contemporaries. Austen Chamberlain was 'the man who always played the game and always lost', not really unfair to the worshipper of Mussolini. Neville Chamberlain was 'a good town clerk in a bad year', a remark which is at least as revealing about Churchill's contempt for administrative reform as it is about Chamberlain. The description of Ramsay MacDonald as 'the boneless wonder' was so grossly unfair that it should now be expunged altogether from memory.

Let us at least say this on behalf of Baldwin and MacDonald: the quality of their leadership was not noticeably poorer than that of the Balfour of whom the Conservatives rid themselves in 1910, or of the Asquith who so signally failed to meet the challenge of war. And one might add that on almost every issue outside foreign affairs on which Churchill voiced a strong opinion, that opinion was misconceived and obscurantist. But these are negative defences. While it is true that MacDonald, Baldwin, and even Neville Chamberlain, represent much that is most constructive and generous in the twenties, it is equally true that none gave the country great leadership.

The fall of the Lloyd George Coalition was, in general, caused by Conservative discontent under what they still regarded as an alien yoke, and, in particular, by the fears aroused by the Prime Minister's handling of the Chanak see p. 62. crisis. Conservative discontent was represented and canalized by Stanley Baldwin, 'a countrified business man who seemed to have reached the Cabinet by accident.' (Actually Baldwin owed his rise to the post of President of the Board of Trade more to his family connexions with Bonar Law than to accident.) Having carefully prepared the ground in advance, Baldwin was able to persuade his party at a meeting held in the Carlton Club on 19th October, 1922, to come out of the Coalition. A number of influential Conservatives, including Austen Chamberlain, resisted this decision, but 1922 has been regarded as a sufficiently auspicious date in Conservative history for it to provide a title for the present-day committee of Conservative back-benchers.

In the general election which followed the Carlton Club decision the Conservatives polled 347, the Lloyd George Liberals 57, and the Asquithians 60. Labour with 142 seats had taken a big step towards office. The reaction against the war was now telling in its favour, and Ramsay MacDonald returned to parliament enveloped by a halo of historical justification, to be again elected leader of the party.

In May, 1923, ill health brought about the resignation of the Prime Minister, Bonar Law, and an interesting constitutional problem. The choice of Prime Minister rested (and still rests) with the Monarch, who should, however, avail himself of the best advice available, and should try to find the man most acceptable to the House of Commons. In 1923 the brightest star in the Conservative firmament was the Marquis Curzon, former Viceroy of India: Lord Curzon's succession was widely expected, not least by Curzon himself. It was, however, pointed out to George V by Balfour, that it would not be fair to the Labour opposition, who had practically no representation in the House of Lords, to have a Prime Minister in that chamber. The King therefore sent for Baldwin who had meantime risen to the office of Chancellor of the Exchequer. Constitutional precedents of this sort do not have the force of absolute law, but it has now become a clear convention of the British Constitution that no peer can expect to become Prime Minister.

Curzon described his successful rival as 'a man of the utmost insignificance', but Curzon had no understanding of the basis of the successes of Stanley Baldwin. Baldwin, though often lazy in seeking their fulfilment, was a man of strong Christian principles. His simple eloquence was well adapted to this age of mass communication, and thus he was able to impress his moral earnestness upon a people who were sick and tired of rhetorical heroics and Welsh wizardry. Speaking at Oxford, Baldwin revealed the theoretical basis of his toryism: 'there is nothing else for this generation to do than devote itself as no other generation has done in the past to the betterment of its millions of people who have not had our advantages'. Baldwin had wide support in the community as a whole, while he was at no time free of the hostility of some of the most powerful elements in his own party.

We have seen how the necessities of war had sullied the pure waters of free trade. There had long been a strong body of opinion in the Conservative party in favour of Tariff Reform, that is to say, wholesale protection. In November, 1923, Baldwin, announcing the conversion of the Government to this policy, sought the endorsement of the country in a second general election in little over a year. 'Suicide during a temporary fit of insanity,' was Philip Snowden's verdict on a decision which produced the following results: Conservatives 259, Labour 191, Liberals 159. The Conservatives no longer had an absolute majority in the House of Commons and the way was open to the formation of the first Labour Government in January, 1924.

Labour was in a difficult position: not only was it in a minority in the House of Commons, but it had achieved a popular vote of less than $4\frac{1}{2}$ millions out of a total poll of $14\frac{1}{2}$ millions. Although the Liberals would do nothing to keep the Conservatives in office, and therefore to this extent helped Labour, their attitude was revealingly expressed by Asquith: 'It is we who govern,' he said. For the Conservatives, Austen Chamberlain remarked, 'a Labour Government would be too weak to do much harm but not too weak to get discredited.' However, there was no question of Labour not taking office; that would be to forfeit its claim to stand as one of the two major parties of State. But what policies should the Government pursue when in office? The left argued in favour of 'living dangerously', of introducing full-blooded Socialist measures and daring the Liberals to throw them out. However, there was little chance of this advice being heeded, for Labour's leaders, MacDonald and Snowden, were both essentially moderates.

The choosing of the Cabinet was left entirely to MacDonald, which was in accord with constitutional practice, though Labour people had long attacked this system as undemocratic. The end product was perhaps as sound as the available talent made possible: former Liberals were rather over-represented, trade unionists under-represented. The inclusion of Lord Haldane, who had been a member of the Labour party right back as far as 1922, as Lord Chancellor, and of two Conservatives, H. P. Macmillan as Lord Advocate, and Lord Chelmsford at the Admiralty, showed that MacDonald was a little too keen that his Government should seem acceptable to top people. Of the left, there were only two representatives: John Wheatley, who was quite the most able of the 'Clydeside Group' of MPs, and Fred Jowett, who, as MacDonald probably knew, was a well-loved, but not particularly vigorous, I L P traditionalist from Bradford.

The two main issues upon which Labour had fought the election were unemployment and foreign policy. On the former, as we noted in Chapter Five, it had failed to equip itself with an economic policy, and its record in office was not a distinguished one: on foreign policy, as we saw in the previous chapter, its record was rather better.

The 1918 Constitution had given the Labour party a specifically Socialist objective. Nationalization was mentioned in the Election Manifesto, and some candidates made much of it, others little. In the event the Labour Government made no attempt at, or preparation for, nationalizing any industry, and Snowden's budget reflected Gladstonian rather than Socialist principles.

In the eyes of the respectable, the Government's greatest sin was the recognition of Soviet Russia, followed up eventually, thanks to the concerted action of a little group of left-wing back-benchers, by a trade agreement. It is against the background of the Russian negotiations that the rather trivial Campbell Case, which brought the downfall of the Government, must be set; so also with the Zinoviev Letter, the rather smelly bone of contention which was flung into the midst of the ensuing general election. The letter (or rather the copies of it – no original was ever seen), purporting to be from the President of the Communist International to the British Communist Party, neatly associated support for the Russian treaty with the prospect of revolution in Britain. The left as a whole denounced the document as a forgery, but MacDonald caused his followers great embarrassment by apparently accepting its genuineness.

In the election the Conservatives re-established an overall majority, though Labour's popular vote continued to advance: the Liberals suffered drastically. The 'Red Letter Scare' probably did not materially affect the results; one Glasgow Socialist MP explained how he successfully dealt with questioners on the subject: 'Ah jist drooned them in a sea of words.' It did, however, along with the Campbell case, arouse doubts as to MacDonald's competence as leader. But the plain fact was, there simply was no one else. And the vast mass of the Labour party still pinned its hopes to the man who had done so much to build up the Labour movement, and whose leonine presence and organ voice gave him an emotive power greater by far, even, than that of Baldwin. Even James Maxton, the colourful leader of the Clydeside ILP group, silenced a demand at the 1925 ILP Conference for a deeper probing into MacDonald's part in the Zinoviev affair.

With his return to office Baldwin brought tranquillity. He said of the gathering troubles in the trade union world, 'we, at least, are not going to fire the first shot'. In an attempt to foster Conservative reunion he gave Churchill (who had now finally left the Liberals) the Exchequer, and Austen Chamberlain the Foreign Office. As we have seen, Baldwin failed to meet the challenge of the chaotic coal industry, but when the General Strike passed off so briefly and effortlessly the country regarded Baldwin as its saviour. In the Trades Disputes Act of 1927, the Prime Minister, truckling to his right-wing

extremists, fired, if not the first shot, a massive and unnecessary bombardment at the trade union movement.

To its credit the Government had the settlement of the
tricky Irish boundary question, left outstanding by the 1921
treaty; the measures of 'tory socialism' mentioned in Chapter
Five; and the Act of 1928 giving all women over twenty-one
the vote. Politically the country was now a full democracy,
though the anomaly which gave two votes to business men and
university graduates remained.

But by 1929 the Ministry described by the *New Statesman*
as the 'most inefficient and laziest of modern governments' –
though attacked by Lord Rothermere from the opposite pole
as 'semi-socialistic' – was fraying badly. The Labour successes (287 seats to the Conservatives' 261) in the 1929
election were not unexpected. Labour still had no overall
majority: the Liberals, putting in, as it proved, their last full-
scale electoral challenge, held the balance with their 59 seats.
A second Labour Government, however, was formed. For the
first time a woman attained Cabinet office: Margaret Bondfield
became Minister of Labour.

More than ever, the overriding issue was unemployment.
Once again a Labour Government in office proved itself no
more able to deal with this problem than the avowedly
capitalist party. This is the first clue to the sudden end of the
Government in August, 1931. Popular novelists have found
ready-made drama in the translation of MacDonald, overnight
as it were, from Labour leader to leader of an overwhelmingly
Conservative 'National' Ministry. How did this come about?
Two trains of circumstances are involved: first the state of
disruption in the British party system in the late twenties, and,
second, the deepening world economic crisis. A final factor
was the psychology of the principal figures involved.

The election results of 1929, we have seen, were, as in
1923, indeterminate: the Liberals, though fighting for their
lives, held an important central position. But the essence of
the party system discussed at the beginning of the chapter is
that the elector should be presented with two clear choices;
the choice is narrow, but at least he can see what he is voting

for, can see whether or not this is carried out, and can give clear notice to quit if he does not like what he sees. In 1929 this system seemed to be falling into chaos; furthermore the two largest parties were suffering from internal disarray. In the Labour party the I L P militants formed themselves into what was in fact an independent group, frequently opposed to the Government; and Sir Oswald Mosley left the Government to form his New Party. On the other side Baldwin was faced with opposition from influential Conservatives, and from rank and filers who blamed him for twice leading them to electoral defeat.

Thus we find throughout the second Labour Government spokesmen from both sides of the house talking in terms of bringing an end to 'party bickering' (Snowden), and of the House acting as a Council of State (MacDonald, Worthington-Evans). The eventual outcome, then, was not wholly a surprise.

The Wall Street financial crash came at the end of October, 1929, but the British economic situation did not start to become acute till early 1931. The Liberals did not have to twist Snowden's arm to get him to set up an ominously orthodox Economy Committee under Sir George May. As soon as Parliament rose for the summer recess the Committee reported. Its unnecessary gloom served to accelerate the crisis. Gold now began to pour from the country, and the position became so serious that on 11th August MacDonald returned to Westminster from his home town of Lossiemouth where he was holidaying. This marks the beginning of the twelve days of crisis proper.

The basic concern of the Bank of England and of the politicians (and there was, with the full knowledge of the Labour Cabinet, consultation between the political leaders) was a restoration of confidence through drastic Government economy. The crux for the Labour Cabinet eventually proved to be the size of the economies – there was provisional agreement upon economies of £56 million – and the means by which they were to be affected. To tide it over its difficulties the Bank of England was meanwhile trying to raise a loan from the American Bank, J. P. Morgan's. At a final meeting of the Labour Cabinet on the evening of Sunday, 23rd August, word came through from New York that the loan could only be granted if the Government gave an earnest of its grim determination to surmount the crisis in the form of a further economy of £12¼ million, to be raised by a ten per cent reduction in Unemployment Benefits. A majority of the Cabinet were prepared to accept these cuts: a minority, including such key-men as Henderson (Foreign Secretary), Graham (President of the Board of Trade), Clynes (Home Secretary), and Adamson (Scottish Secretary), were not. The Government could not go on.

The normal outcome would have been a Ministry headed by Baldwin, but King George V, acting not wisely, perhaps, but with complete constitutional propriety – and this illustrates the central importance of the Crown in time of political crisis – persuaded MacDonald to head a 'National' Government. Here the personal factors came into play: on MacDonald's side, his vanity and aristocratic sense of indispensability, his detachment from the true sentiments of the Labour movement, his love of compromise and the subtle solution, and, it is only fair to add, his sense of duty: and on Baldwin's, his deficiencies in leadership, but eminent suitability for the role of principal adviser.

MacDonald took Snowden, Thomas and Sankey (the Lord Chancellor) with him; he made little effort to win the support of other Labour members. To begin with there was no great bitterness; from one point of view, MacDonald and his dozen followers had acted with complete consistency; from that point of view the Labour Cabinet had run away from the crisis leaving the unemployed almost entirely to the mercies of the Conservatives. Bitterness came when MacDonald, despite a promise to the contrary, went to the country in October. In an unpleasant election in which MacDonald asked for a 'Doctor's Mandate', Snowden turned his venom on his former colleagues, and Runciman started the scare that Labour had designs on the Post Office savings of ordinary people, the National Government built up the mammoth total of 556 seats, while Labour was reduced to a pathetic 46. It was now that tales of MacDonald's 'treachery' began to circulate fiercely; and Labour retired to lick its wounds, and to do some much needed economic thinking.

PHASE III : EXPANSION, 1931-39

CHAPTER EIGHT

PLANNING A WAY OUT

THE Great War revealed the potential of the planned economy; although the twenties provided plenty of evidence of the deficiencies of unmanaged capitalism in decline, this potential was scarcely realized before 1931. It was the great economic and political crisis which provided the necessary psychological snap, pointing clearly to the need for a more thorough abandonment of economic traditions and bringing the concept of 'planning' right into the foreground of the nation's consciousness. Putting the case for planning in his *Reconstruction*, published in 1933, Harold Macmillan, then a leader of the younger progressive Conservatives, concluded:

> Planning is forced upon us, therefore, not for idealistic reasons, but because the old mechanism which served us when markets were expanding naturally and spontaneously is no longer adequate when the tendency is in the opposite direction. (p. 18.)

Other symptoms of this new emphasis were the establishment by a group of business men and civil servants of the independent research organization, Political and Economic Planning, and the publication of *Recovery*, by Sir Arthur (now Lord) Salter, and of *Britain's Political Future*, by Lord Allen of Hurtwood (the Clifford Allen of the ILP and NCF, he had been one of MacDonald's few Labour supporters in the 1931 crisis). Allen and Macmillan were the brains behind the inter- and extra-party group which in 1935 published *The Next Five Years*, a blue print for Government action over the life-span of one parliament. That same year the ever-green Lloyd George launched, in his Council of Action, a similar movement, though with a more definite political emphasis. By 1936 the planners were on a firm, dry footing with the completion of the great Keynesian economic structure through the publication of the *Treatise on Money* (1930) and his *General Theory* (1936).

While the domestic condition of Britain was clearly the basic factor in this vogue for planning, it is true also that the various economic experiments being carried on in other lands had a strong impact. Allen pointed particularly at the achievements of Roosevelt's New Deal; Macmillan had been impressed by a visit paid to the Soviet Union. Indeed Russia's large-scale economic planning captured the imagination of many who had previously been among her strongest critics. Significant converts were Sydney and Beatrice Webb, as can be seen from their *Soviet Communism, a New Civilization?* (the question mark was dropped from the second edition), and the historian Sir Bernard Pares, who published his *Moscow Admits a Critic* in 1936.

The planners had great faith in the potential of science. Allen and Macmillan regarded the distinguished zoologist Julian (now Sir Julian) Huxley, author *inter alia* of *Essays in Popular Science* (1926), as one of their most precious collaborators (Allen's private correspondence is full of pleas to Huxley not to let pressure of work bring about his resignation from the Group). In the thirties F. G. Hopkins, now a grand old man of science, became a leading publicist for the exploitation of science for the social good. He was one of the first to advocate the creation of a Ministry of Science.

While the country's best brains were evolving the social and economic canons which all parties were to accept in the forties and fifties, what was the Government of the day doing to promote recovery? Unemployment continued to rise till January 1933 when it was just short of 3 millions. Thereafter it dropped to under 2·5 millions in August, to under 2 millions in July 1935, and to 1·6 million one year later. At this level (still a full 12 per cent) it remained steady for the rest of the decade. Exports made only a fractional recovery after 1932, but our share of a declining world trade rose slightly. By 1936 imports were back at the 1929 level and were costing us

32 per cent less. Three industries which did make striking advances were steel, housing and chemicals. The steel industry actually opened new plants, though away from the depressed areas; production rose steadily till by 1937 it was 50 per cent up on 1929. Low costs, local authority encouragement, low interest rates, and the growth of the Building Societies, all helped to foster a housing boom, with an average figure for England and Wales of between 300,000 and 350,000 houses per annum, as opposed to an average of 150,000 per annum in the previous ten years.

Most important of all, from the point of view of the growth of contemporary British society, was the expansion in the pharmaceuticals branch of the chemical industry. The primary factor here was the revolutionary scientific advance embodied in the development after 1935 of the sulpha-drugs. Henceforth the pharmaceuticals firms were to find that in order to keep abreast of the times it was essential to maintain large-scale research establishments. As Professor Ritchie Calder has put it (in *The Life-Savers*) 'research had caused an expansion of industry, and industry had caused an expansion of research'. In terms of actual employment figures the effects, of course, were not great; but this is one of the fundamental stages in the increasingly scientific orientation of British industry.

In general economic activity Britain's position in the thirties does contrast very favourably with that of such other countries as the United States and France. For this the National Government can take at least some credit, though in the main its policies were fortuitous, or just irrelevant. Fundamental to British recovery were the general picking up of world trade after 1933, and the circumstance that world prices of primary products remained low, thus favouring an industrial country like Britain. Low prices meant a fall in the cost of living, so that money was freed for investment; and Britain had greater investment opportunities than other countries because of the failure to exploit them in the twenties. The slow revival of industry, the continued development of new industries, and the remarkable expansion of service (laundering, entertainment, etc.) and tertiary (distribution, commerce, government, etc.) industries, meant more jobs, and therefore greater demand for goods, which further assisted recovery. After 1936, too, the rearmament boom had a similar effect.

The National Government had been formed to restore confidence, balance the budget, and maintain the Gold Standard. One of its first acts was to go off the Gold Standard ('No one told us we could do *that*', a former Labour minister, Hugh Dalton, lamented). It thus unwittingly stumbled upon an important remedy: the consequent devaluation of the pound assisted exports, and the mild bout of inflation fostered economic expansion. But the ostensible policy of the new Government was one of severe economy, a policy both harsh and, as Keynes pointed out, economically 'replete with folly'; however, what was in effect an unbalanced budget in 1932 meant that the inflationary trend outbid the deflationary one. It is one of the prime justifications for the formation of this Government that while its right hand maintained the respectable front necessary for business confidence, its left hand surreptitiously permitted the unorthodox policies which were in fact needed for recovery. Two Keynesian theses were openly adopted. From 6 per cent the Bank Rate was reduced to 2 per cent, where it remained till the outbreak of war: cheap money naturally facilitated investment. Secondly, in July 1932, the Exchange Equalization Fund was established: by means of what was in effect a managed currency it was hoped to iron out the worst strains resulting from international monetary fluctuations.

Upon this rather hesitantly laid groundwork of Government fiscal control was built up an elaborate, and on the whole effective edifice of quotas, marketing schemes, and subsidies. The Milk Marketing Board, to take but one example, was established in 1933; here was the beginning of the road to the era of the Pinta Milka Day. Subsidies to agriculture had an immediate beneficial effect on output (another decade and a great war were to pass before subsidies began to loom in people's eyes as 'feather bedding' for indolent farmers); subsidies to shipping were less successful. The Government even ventured further into the realm of nationalization, for this was what was in fact involved in the establishment, in 1932, of the London Passenger Transport Board, and in 1939, of the British Overseas Airways Corporation; in 1938 an Act for the Nationalization of Coal Royalties was passed.

The great economic innovation of the decade, of course, was the final abandonment of Free Trade. The key measure was Neville Chamberlain's Import Duties Act of 1932, which established a full-scale system of protective tariffs. A Conference at Ottawa later in the year was to decide on the matter of Imperial preferences; this Conference was not a striking success and such decisions as were taken were rather to the advantage of the Dominions than of the home country. However, whatever the Dominions gained in the thirties, they more than amply repaid during the Second World War.

What, meantime, was private industry doing?

The trend towards combination and concentration continued, now masked by the respectable title of rationalization. As in the war, active encouragement was provided by the Government, which, for instance, backed the formation in 1934 of the British Iron and Steel Federation and its subsequent agreements with the International Steel Cartel. The expansion in steel we have noted; in the main the tale was of closures. In the name of rationalization the great Mossend works at Coatbridge in Scotland were shut down, and sudden economic death was visited on the town of Dowlais, once the proud centre of the Welsh iron industry. A similar policy in regard to shipping was followed by the National Shipbuilders' Security. Together these two industrial ogres were responsible for the 'murder' of the Tyneside town of Jarrow.

From all this it is obvious that many of the people of the country were no better off in the thirties than in the twenties, and some were worse off. In 1934 the Government was moved to do something about areas like Jarrow, the Scottish Lowlands, South Wales, and the other heavy industrial centres; but its Depressed Areas Act proved pitifully inadequate. Scottish discontent burst out in a resurgence of Scottish nationalism, which was scarcely assuaged by the modest devolution implied in the establishment of a Government headquarters at St

Andrew's House in Edinburgh in 1939. There was a similar movement in Wales, whose unemployment level was 16 per cent above the United Kingdom average. Organized hunger marches, often rather brutally dealt with by the police, became a feature of the London scene, and permanent human wastage seemed an immutable law in the older industrial areas.

Although the amenities of life, including public health, continued to improve, surveys conducted in the thirties showed that much of the nation was still undernourished; Sir John Boyd Orr suggested in 1936 that 10 per cent of the population (including 20 per cent of the nation's children) was very badly fed, and as much as 50 per cent ill-fed. Army medical tests helped to bear out this estimate. The 1931 economies had involved the 10 per cent cut in unemployment benefits, and the imposition of a Means Test, which, in itself unpleasant in principle, was too often the excuse for bureaucratic niggardliness. For those in work there was a slight rise in real wages towards the end of the period and there were good wages to be earned in the newer industries in the south. Thus the general population trend is a reversal of that of the early industrial revolution: there is now a marked shift back towards the south, with a concentration in the Home Counties, especially in the London suburbs and in towns like Slough.

This trend coincided with the great expansion in motor-car production – there were over a million cars on British roads by 1930. The new London suburbs such as Hendon were served in part by extensions of the Underground (in fact built over ground). But the flow of commuters from home to office in the morning, and from office to home in evening, more than hinted at the traffic problems which were to be a serious reality after the Second World War. As buses and cars crawled along the main roads, ribbons of semi-detached houses, petrol stations, and cafés kept them company. The British urban pattern was changing: instead of congested slums for some there was to be congested roads for all.

Bad housing was one of the worst legacies of nineteenth-century industrial growth. Despite the housing boom, Britain in the thirties was still disfigured by areas of chronic overcrowding, and insanitary slums. Provision for slum clearance was made in Acts of 1930 and 1935, but the problem remained basically unchanged, to emerge festering and swollen from the incubation of the Second World War. The new emphasis on aesthetic standards and the vogue for planning is well illustrated in the comprehensive Town and Country Planning Act of 1932, which consolidated legislation of 1909, 1925 and 1929; though this Act was an important step forward, there was still less than 5 per cent of the nation's land under planning control at the end of the decade.

The movement towards a welfare state continued. Although the Unemployment Act of 1934, and the Unemployment Assistance Board (with a Means Test) which it set up, was widely unpopular, it was in fact an important step towards bringing administrative order into this aspect of social security. An Act of 1937 brought the black-coated workers into the framework of the original Lloyd George Insurance Act. The imposition of tariffs, and reductions in direct taxation in the 1934 budget, were regressive changes in the tax structure, but in 1937 Neville Chamberlain, frequently attacked from the right for being too 'socialistic' – as indeed was the whole National Government – introduced a 5 per cent tax on business profits.

The trade union movement continued in decline until 1933 when, at 4,392,000, its membership was little above that of 1913; there now followed a recovery, so that on the eve of World War II the figure was close on 6 millions. On the whole the movement was characterized by a growing respectability: two of its leaders, Pugh and Citrine, were knighted in 1935. It was the latter who enunciated at the 1938 TUC Conference the principle that 'in dealing with any Government on behalf of the trade union movement its conduct must be determined by industrial and political considerations'. That is to say the TUC would deal directly with any Government in power rather than try specifically to act through the Labour Party. As with so many other features of the 1930's, this was the forerunner of the attitude which, on the whole, prevailed after 1945.

CHAPTER NINE

THE DECADE OF COMMITMENT

IN 1936 Geoffrey Gorer published a satirical novel under the title *Nobody Talks Politics*. The action opens in 1924 with the hero, Freddie Green, at a party redolent of the irresponsible, apolitical political atmosphere of the gay twenties. He is bitten by a lemur and falls asleep for ten years. In 1934 Freddie is in a different world: *everybody* is talking politics. The contrast is a fundamental one. Things had been too bad for too long, the 1931 crisis had been too serious for anyone to ignore: Britain turned in upon herself, and the work of her great intellectual figures reflects their profound concern with the social and political problems of the day. That is to say, they are 'committed'.

It is not suggested that the writers of the thirties were necessarily particularly successful in commanding a wider audience (it is often said that they were simply speaking to an empty room). The commercialization and exploitation of the new mass culture continued, yet this stimulating decade does also show a definite expansion of minority culture, and perhaps even some sort of coming together of the two, rather than any increased divergence.

In addition to the economic situation there were two other main impulses behind commitment. The crushing dominance obtained by the National Government in the 1931 election induced an orientation towards extreme political courses, in place of a previous vague sympathy for the now hopelessly depleted Labour or Liberal parties. Secondly there was the question of the rise of Nazism abroad and of Fascism (the British Union of Fascists was founded in 1934) at home. Extreme leftism seemed the only possible counterpoise.

Seen in this light, the strong pull of Communism upon the British intellectuals is not surprising. (Predictably, the final section of *Nobody Talks Politics* is really a demonstration of the necessity of Communism.) From the grip of Communism upon the intellectuals there followed the tendency to see the world situation in the simplified terms of absolute German evil and absolute Russian purity. In the Spanish Civil War, which broke out in 1936, the struggle of the Spanish Government, aided (apparently) by Russia, against the Franco rebels, aided by Hitler and Mussolini, crystallized these attitudes: it seemed the very embodiment of the fight of right against wrong. Spain in fact was to provide the occasion and the imagery for some of the best poetry of the thirties.

It is with poetry that we shall begin. In 1933 the critic Hugh Gordon Porteous commented dryly, 'Verse will be worn longer this year, and rather Red'. Of the three leading poets W. H. Auden, Stephen Spender and C. Day Lewis, only the last was actually a Communist party member, but all were committed. Lewis points a withering finger at the members of the National Government:

> Consider these, for we have condemned them
> Leaders to no sure land . . .

Then an obvious reference to one of Baldwin's most famous speeches: 'They pray for peace, they hand down disaster'. The only solution is, 'The break with the past, the major operation', that is to say, Communist revolution.

In the prologue to their verse play, *The Dog beneath the Skin*, Auden and Christopher Isherwood record the condition of the countryside. Of the depressed areas Auden had written:

> Get there if you can and see the land you once were proud to own,
> Though the roads have almost vanished the expresses never run:
> Smokeless chimneys, damaged bridges, rotting wharves, and choked canals, . . .

One of the finest aspects of twentieth-century scepticism has been the rise of a rational Scottish nationalism in place of the blustering Burns and Haggis sycophancy of the late nine-teenth century. The prophet of the 'Scottish Renaissance' was Hugh McDiarmid, whose motto (and it would serve for most of the writers of the time) was a phrase of Thomas Hardy's: 'literature is the written expression of revolt against accepted things.' McDiarmid had joined the Communist party long before the intellectuals of the thirties, and he remained behind when they left. His *First Hymn to Lenin* (1931), in fact, anticipates the general poetic flirtation with Communism. The cultural revival in Wales was based solidly on the National Eisteddfod and on the four colleges of the University of Wales. Even so, there could be no stemming the decline in the per-centage of the population speaking Welsh.

The seriousness of the age, and the fact that the serious appeal went far beyond the confines of intellectual coteries, are clear in the success of the Left Book Club, and, most significant and successful of all, the founding in 1935 of Penguin Books. The growth in production and popularity of paper-back books was to be one of the most interesting and encouraging trends in the period after the Second World War. Meanwhile there were other popular works of a serious nature published in hard covers. Lancelot Hogben produced his *Mathematics for the Million*, part of his series of 'Primers for the Age of Plenty'. Tom Harrisson, along with Charles Madge and Humphrey Jennings and countless willing assistants, pioneered the application of anthropological methods to the study of the behaviour of the modern Briton: Mass Observa-tion was both a symptom of the times and a portent of the future; the first fruits of its application to politics (psephology is now a science) was the return, in a by-election at Fulham, of Dr Edith Summerskill.

Artists, too, tended towards political purpose and social realism, and this was expressed in the formation in 1933 of the Artists International Association. There was still a rage for 'isms', though generally the same list of names appeared each time. One short-lived group, the Objective Abstractionists (called by their opponents the Objectionable Obstructionists), contained many of the painters who, in their own right, came to the fore in the forties: Richards, Pasmore, Hitchens among them.

Undoubtedly the most striking artistic movement of the time was surrealism. The International Surrealist Exhibition of the summer of 1936 attracted 20,000 people, again suggesting that the arts were now achieving a wider appeal. Although many of the surrealists sought identification with the revolutionary cause, it was felt by their grimmer colleagues that their emphasis on the incongruous and the world of dreams unqualified them for the serious task. Herbert Read canvassed the serious purposes of surrealism in an introduction to the International Exhibition:

Do not judge this movement kindly. It is not just another amusing stunt. It is defiant – the desperate act of men too profoundly convinced of the rottenness of our civilization to want to save a shred of its respectability.

Paul Nash was the only surrealist of stature that Britain managed to produce. More evidence of the extension of artistic aims to society as a whole is to be found in the Art in Industry Exhibition of 1935.

In architecture the thirties applied the innovations of Le Corbusier and Gropius with greater sanity, and therefore greater aesthetic effect, than had the twenties: among the successes of the period were the Stratford-on-Avon Memorial Theatre, the *Daily Express* Building in Fleet Street, Battersea Power Station, and the London University Senate House. Thirties architecture appeared at its worst in the chains of fussily modernistic cinemas built by the new combines, Odeon, ABC, and Gaumont British.

The music renaissance continued. Ballet, the musical art-form most related to the expressionistic trends of the times, enjoyed a great revival, and the Sadler's Wells Theatre was reopened in 1931 as a new shrine for *balletomanes* (a significant new coinage of the period). The exotic nature of opera (of which Samuel Johnson once complained) was emphasized by the birth in 1934 of the exclusive Glyndebourne Opera, a happy event from the point of view of operatic standards, but less happy in its re-emphasis on the narrowness of minority culture. Much more auspicious, in the wider context, was the foundation in 1930 of the BBC Symphony Orchestra, which catered for, and created, a greater audience than ever before for classical music.

Not all the writers and artists of the period, naturally, fit into the same pattern. George Orwell, who was less than adulatory in his attitude towards the working class, and who exposed the unpleasant realities of Communist activity in Spain, was very much an odd man out, and was only accorded full critical approval after 1945. On the other hand the Edwardian giant, Bernard Shaw, whose prolific output had continued all through the twenties, was already coming to be regarded with the detachment suitable to accepted genius, rather than as a lively commentator on the contemporary scene; yet there were obvious references to the great political crisis in his *On the Rocks*. In 1928, H. G. Wells had hinted at the ideas subsequently embraced by the 'planners' of the thirties in his *The Open Conspiracy*; in 1933 he issued a substantially revised version of this work.

Even among the popular novelists there is a deliberate attention to social and political problems. Such books as Walter Greenwood's *Love on the Dole* and J. B. Priestley's *Angel Pavement* did much to awaken people to the condition of Britain. The early novels of Graham Greene had a strong sense of social anger. *It's a Battlefield* concerns the fate of a bus driver called Drover who has killed a policeman during an anti-Fascist demonstration in Hyde Park; protest is expressed through the thoughts of the Police Commissioner:

. . . the Commissioner was more than ever thankful that justice was not his business. He knew quite well the cause of the discrepancy; the laws were made by property owners in defence of property; that was why a Fascist could talk treason without prosecution; that was why a man who defrauded the State in defence of his private wealth did not even lose the money he had gained; that was why Drover could not so easily be reprieved – he was a Communist. (p. 229.)

With *Brighton Rock*, Greene began a series of Catholic problem novels, illumined by a sharp eye for the contemporary scene. His success, and that of Evelyn Waugh, is further evidence of the continued Catholic revival. The great thriller writer of the twenties had been Edgar Wallace; now there was a craze for the sophisticated detective story, always posing a balanced conundrum of skilfully laid clues, often written by an intellectual eminent in another field (Dorothy Sayers or G. D. H. Cole, say), and sometimes full of literary, or arty, or simply Latin, tags.

British films continued to be generally poor in quality, though they benefited from the talents of continental exiles like Alexander Korda, whose *Private Life of Henry VIII* was the one great pre-war British film success. Under the influence of Grierson and Cavalcanti, there were, however, important advances in the documentary. With the expansion of broadcasting there came a revival of music-hall variety in an up-to-date style: the singer Gracie Fields became the great star of popular entertainment. Towards the end of the decade Radio Luxembourg, financed from advertisement revenue, and providing a popular alternative to what was still regarded as the rather staid BBC, was founded. This development must simply be accounted a part of the growth of the commercialized mass culture which had begun in the twenties.

The popularity of the great spectator sports, products of later Victorian Britain, reached a peak in the thirties. Over the cricket contest with Australia, there blew up an international controversy: England's not very gentlemanly tactics were widely characterised as 'body-line bowling', which they were, though described by their practitioners by the innocuous title of 'leg-theory'. On another occasion a visit of Royalty had such shattering effects on an eminent Australian batsman that he popped up an easy catch to the English captain, Walter Hammond; the scorer, equally shattered, made the following entry: *Ponsford, c. Hammond b. George V*, 81.

The hopelessness born of chronic economic depression not unnaturally quickened the British gambling spirit, and it was in the thirties that football pools became a major industry. Economic insecurity was perhaps also reflected in the fact that the consumption of cigarettes rose, while that of beer fell slightly. For all the poverty and insecurity, however, the holiday habit was catching on: in the context of the new trade union respectability and general amicability of industrial relations, holidays with pay became an accepted notion. Again the theory of mass tended to prevail and such promoters as Billy Butlin began to make provision for bulk holiday-making in their vast holiday camps. Fresh air became something of a fetish; hiking became widely popular and in 1930 the Youth Hostels Movement was imported from Germany. Ownership of the motor-car slowly became more widely diffused, and in 1934 came the first hesitant steps towards road safety, with the institution of the driving-test, and the installation of Belisha beacons.

In fashion there was a tendency towards brightness and informality in men's clothes. With women there was something of a Victorian revival (a counterpart in a way of the thirties' return to seriousness); certainly a restoration of femininity, in which the concept of *it* was replaced by that of *oomph*.

The country was now firmly attached to its monarchy. The celebrated Christmas Day broadcasts were begun in 1932, and the Jubilee of 1935, and the Coronation of George VI in 1937 were celebrated with great pomp and popular rejoicing. In between had come the brief reign of Edward VIII. The fact that he was forced to abdicate because of his insistence upon marrying a divorcee, Mrs Simpson, illustrates the persistence in modern Britain of many of the moral canons of mid-Victorian England. A. P. Herbert's Divorce Act of the following year did represent a slight relaxation in that it allowed insanity and cruelty as grounds for divorce.

How were these social changes reflected in the newspaper Press, the lifeblood of any modern culture? First of all advertising had now at last broken free from its nineteenth-century conventions, and was beginning to present its contemporary uninhibited form. Advertising played its part in the great circulation war which marked the first few years of the decade. The new *Daily Herald*, with the vast publishing potential of

Odhams behind it, was able to lead off with the stupendous offer to regular readers of sixteen volumes of Dickens, worth four guineas, for eleven shillings. The *Mail*, the *Express*, and the *News Chronicle*, now sent into the field a vast array of canvassers offering goods ranging from encyclopaedias to silk stockings to anyone who would undertake to take their paper. It was reckoned that you could clothe a family by judiciously swopping from paper to paper. When at last the war was over the *Express* was seen to have emerged as the giant of the British popular Press: its circulation of over 2 millions was the largest in the world. The *Herald* soon lost its initial impetus and but for the war would probably have found itself once more in serious difficulties.

There was undoubtedly a lowering of standards in this new circulation race, though whether these standards could really be said to be any worse than those of the essentially similar papers which had catered for the Victorian lower middle class is debatable. On the positive side it can be recorded that more and more people than ever before were reading newspapers. No doubt one of the things which most attracted them was the advent of the gossip columnist, usually, as for example with William Hickey of the *Express*, not a single journalist but a team of highly skilled dustbin riflers. In the gossip columns were featured such sensational matter as the matrimonial affairs of the romantic aviators, Mollison and Amy Johnson, the aberrations of the Rector of Stiffkey, and the latest movements of the Loch Ness Monster, another discovery of the thirties. Particularly unfortunate was such mollycoddling of the readership as the *Express*'s bland denial of the possibility of war a few weeks before its outbreak.

The twentieth-century newspaper revolution was completed with the launching in 1935 by H. G. Bartholomew of a new *Daily Mirror* on the tabloid pattern hitherto confined to America. These journalistic developments would seem to have little to do with commitment or the wider spread of a higher culture. Yet Bartholomew's *Mirror*, along with the gossip and the pin-ups, had an unmistakable radicalism which was in itself a part of the tradition of the thirties, and which had remarkable effects on the 1945 general election. In 1938, furthermore, came the establishment of *Picture Post*, which met the thirtyish demand for up-to-date pictorial treatment of serious current problems. Even *Woman*, launched by Odhams in 1937, to begin with, had a radical twinge. Admittedly this did not last long, but the growth of the mass circulation women's magazines, of which *Woman* was the first and most successful, was a cardinal feature of the post-1945 world, and a culmination of one aspect of women's rise to power in the community.

All in all it might not unreasonably be said of the decade of commitment that although Auden, Spender, and the others had little genuine contact with the society with which they so ardently wished to associate themselves, although the trend towards exploitation of the second-rate and the lowest interests of the greatest number, continued, the general picture was of a growth of enlightened cultural activity rather than any definite hardening of the division between mass and minority.

CHAPTER TEN

THE MINISTRY OF NONE OF THE TALENTS

THE general election of October, 1931, was in part brought about by Conservative lust after Tariff Reform. Unhappily the National Government contained such rigid Free Traders as Snowden and those Liberals who followed the leads of Samuel and Sinclair. Thus, to begin with, the Cabinet publicly 'agreed to differ', a quaint perversion of the constitutional practice of joint Cabinet responsibility. With the signing of the Ottawa Agreements, however, the Free Traders left the Government, so that it was now almost a pure Conservative Ministry. This was merely underlined when MacDonald, whose faculties were beginning to give way under the strain of a lifetime of overwork, swopped places with Baldwin in June, 1935. A year later, J. H. Thomas resigned after a budget indiscretion, and in May, 1937, Baldwin, basking in an Indian summer of glory evoked by his tactful handling of the Abdication crisis, handed over to Neville Chamberlain.

The domestic record of the National Ministries, we have seen, was by no means unrelievedly bad. In his 1934 budget speech Chamberlain was able to boast that the country had come from Bleak House to Great Expectations – this remarkable literary allusion was doubtless stimulated by the *Daily Herald* gift offer mentioned in the previous chapter. Unfortunately the greatest challenge of the times came in foreign policy, and the general level of modest ministerial competence did not extend to the talented vigour needed to deal with matters of war and peace. The last hang-over of the optimism of the twenties was the long-prepared-for Disarmament Conference which opened at Geneva in February, 1932, under the presidency of Arthur Henderson, and dragged hopelessly on for over two years. The real end came when Nazi Germany withdrew from the Conference in October, 1933. Paradoxically, despite this blow to hopes of world peace, pacifist sentiment, as we shall see, increased in Britain; in part this was an intensification of the anti-war trends prevalent since the previous world holocaust, an extension of what we have called the forward movement in foreign policy, and in part a reflection of the age's serious devotion to the cause of humanity, and distrust of 'the leaders to no sure land'.

There was a veritable hail of other blows to world peace. In September, 1931, Japan invaded Manchuria; from then till February, 1933, Britain, the United States (which was the other great power most nearly concerned), and the League of Nations (and the League, it cannot be too often emphasized, could do nothing beyond what the powers willed it to do), vacillated upon this clear issue of aggression. Finally after the painstaking Lytton Enquiry, the League condemned Japan who promptly withdrew from membership. And there the matter rested. The Manchurian crisis broke at an awkward time for the new-born Government. It was, as a simple geographical fact, a most awkward one to deal with, and there was certainly no public sentiment in favour of strong action. It was in February, 1933, that the Oxford Union passed the celebrated resolution that 'this House will in no circumstances fight for its King and Country'; and it was in October that a Labour candidate, fighting the pacifist ticket, turned a Conservative majority of 14,521 into a Labour one of 4,840, at the equally publicized East Fulham by-election.

The second blow came from nearer at hand: from Germany, whose Weimar Republic, widely admired in this country for its post-war modishness by such diverse people as Christopher Isherwood, the writer, and the sponsors of the British Youth Hostel movement, gave place in January, 1933, to the Nazi dictatorship of Adolf Hitler. Hitler's first move in his avowed aim of destroying the Versailles Settlement was the open rearmament of his country. While the immediate reaction of the League of Nations was condemnatory, Britain now found that fine spray of confused motives which we discussed in Chapter

Seven blowing back in her eyes: the irony was that the forward movement had so successfully canvassed its ideas that right-wing politicians were now using morally impeccable arguments about the unjustness of our previous treatment of Germany to bolster an unjustifiable softness towards Hitler. The National Government, in the space of as many months, plunged into three mutually contradictory policies.

In March, 1935, a Government White Paper announced the official beginning of rearmament: it seemed that the Government had been stirred by the powerful warnings of Winston Churchill (once again in the political wilderness) into preparing for defence against the dictators. In April a defensive agreement with France and Italy was concluded at Stresa – Mussolini, a dictator with Abyssinian blood on his hands (see below), was apparently a perfectly acceptable ally. Then to crown all a Naval Agreement with Germany herself, which was in flat violation of the undertakings at Stresa, was signed on 4th June.

The Government was inconsistent; the Labour Opposition was perhaps little better in its consistent opposition to rearmament. Labour argued that this right-wing Government, friendly, it seemed, to Hitler and to Mussolini, was not to be trusted with arms; it ignored the fact that collective security could not be enforced without the necessary means. The public at large was perhaps not as unwise as the politicians. In June, 1935, the League of Nations Union published the results of its Peace Ballot – a sort of pioneer Gallup Poll on a huge scale. The conclusion to be drawn from the poll was that there was overwhelming support for the League of Nations (there was an 11 million vote for this) and quite strong support for backing up the League with military action ($6\frac{3}{4}$ million voted for this, $2\frac{1}{2}$ million against). But the effects upon the Baldwin (as it now was) Government were unfortunate. It went all out for a show of giving the electorate what it wanted – support for the League of Nations (in which old-guard Conservatives did not believe); and it decided to play down what it itself believed to be needed – rearmament.

Third in the series of blows to international order was the

Italian attack on Abyssinia which began in December, 1934. Again there was a grain of moral decency in the undignified predicament in which Britain found herself. Britain had long since won her imperial territories, but Mussolini, like the poor little piggy in the nursery saw, had none. This is part at least of the explanation for the deal, involving the cession to Italy of part of British Somaliland, which the new British Foreign Secretary, Sir Samuel Hoare, proposed. The deal fell through, and Hoare now (September, 1935) promised full British backing for the League Covenant. On 7th October, Italy was declared an aggressor by the League of Nations, and economic sanctions (but imperfect ones – oil in particular was excluded) were imposed upon her. There was great enthusiasm at home: at last Britain seemed to be backing the League in what, at first sight, looked like positive action. The Government decided to have an election.

The Labour party was not in good shape. The ILP had in 1932 finally disaffiliated; its rather shadowy successor the Socialist League, dominated by the austere lawyer, Sir Stafford Cripps, proved a doubtful asset in its periodic advocacy of undemocratic courses. Since the débâcle of 1931 the party had been led by the absolute Christian pacifist George Lansbury, but he succumbed at the 1935 Annual Conference to a vicious attack from Ernest Bevin. Clement Attlee was subsequently elected leader, and the party committed itself to the support of sanctions against Italy, but was still unsure on the question of armaments.

Baldwin later admitted that in the October election he had deliberately concealed from the electorate the need for rearmament, though fully intending to carry it out. It is this sort of piddling dishonesty that makes nonsense of the usual defence of the National Government that it gave the country the foreign policy it wanted, and, therefore, the foreign policy (and, eventually, war) which it deserved: the country was not even given the facts. With the election safely won, the Government attempted another deal with Mussolini. However the Hoare-Laval plan became known prematurely, and in the great popular outcry Baldwin discarded Hoare. But sanctions were quietly dropped, for Germany had struck another, and much more menacing blow.

On 7th March, 1936, German troops marched into the Rhineland – a demilitarized area according to the Versailles treaty. This, it has often been said, was the last occasion on which Hitler might have been stopped without world war; certainly the German generals expected immediate Franco-British action. But the British, again suffering from an uneasy conscience, could not help feeling that Germany had simply marched into her own back-garden: what was there to fight about in that? But again there was contradiction: rearmament was intensified.

The Rhineland crisis was rapidly followed by the outbreak of the Spanish Civil War (July, 1936). Despite the readily apparent fact that Germany and Italy were providing the Franco rebels with munitions and men (as Russia was soon assisting the Government) the British Government insisted on the farce of 'non-intervention'. The spectacle of a democratic Government and its supporters being ground mercilessly into the dust by the might of European Fascism, while Britain's rulers refused even to allow the Spanish loyalists to buy arms, called forth in Britain an anger unparalleled since the Bulgarian atrocities, and created a new divide in British society.

Let us consider the two sides of that divide. On the one side lay the old Conservative *élite* who by instinct felt favourably disposed towards authoritarian régimes abroad ('the trains run on time,' was the notorious justification of this class for the Mussolini dictatorship); the big business interests, who, in this particular case, saw Franco as the safest guardian of British commercial interests in Spain; the upper middle-class and the respectable generally, represented by *The Times*, which under the editorship of Geoffrey Dawson angled and suppressed news in the interests of the appeasement of Hitler; and various romantics, spiritual heirs of Sir Walter Scott and the older Wordsworth, who thought in terms of a holy crusade against Communism.

Open Fascism in Britain, stronger, Mr Cross maintains in his *The Fascists in Britain*, than we sometimes like to think, was dying out; it had really reached a peak in the Olympia meeting of 7th June, 1934, at which there had been an unprecedented display of spotlit thuggery. This both the Press and the police (who seemed to adopt a disquietingly tolerant attitude towards the various Blackshirt marches) played down; but the action of individual M.P.s – some of the younger Conservatives played a distinguished part – and members of the public brought the Government up against this problem of the undemocratic challenge to democracy. The answer was sought in two measures: the Incitement to Disaffection Bill of 1934, and the Public Order Bill of 1936. Both were strong meat for a time of peace, but have been referred to as precedents in the recent resurgence of racialism and Fascism in Notting Hill and elsewhere.

Right-wing extremism was one of the factors, consolidated in the hot blast of the Spanish Civil War, helping to make for solidarity on the other side of the divide. Here was to be found a range of people from Liberal readers of the *News Chronicle*, to Communist party card holders; the Independent M.P. Eleanor Rathbone and the Conservative Duchess of Atholl also took a stand against the Government's Spanish policy. Most significant, the middle-of-the-road groups, originally concerned solely with planning and research, were slowly pushed to this side of the divide.

First to issue a direct political challenge was Lloyd George's Council of Action (naturally quickly characterized by opponents as the Council of Faction), a body which may be regarded as representing the last political kick of British nonconformism (long since chased out of the I L P where it had still been strong in the early twenties): of Lloyd George's twelve area organizations, six had as chairmen ministers of religion. Non-political bodies such as the League of Nations Union found themselves increasingly adopting a critical attitude towards the Government. The Next Five Years Group was slower to move: its organ, *The New Outlook*, under the influence of Harold Macmillan, who had now refused the Government whip, was often critical, and was accused by a reader in May, 1937, of becoming 'increasingly dominated by the "Left".' Lord Allen was less sure of the value of expressing direct political opposition to the Government, as opposed to making constructive criticisms of its policies – he felt that no useful combination could be attained on this side of the divide without the support of the Labour party.

Here was the rub. As early as September, 1936, Attlee laid down the law: 'I do not believe in a united front or a Popular Front on any basis except that of Socialism.' It was this official Labour hostility which killed the attempts at an effective union of the anti-Government forces in either a United Front (of left-wing forces only) or a Popular Front (embracing dissident Conservatives as well as leftists). None the less in 1938 such important Labour politicians as Cripps, Trevelyan, Aneurin Bevan, and Strauss, despairing of all normal means of turning the Chamberlain Government from its courses, again advocated a Popular Front, and were duly rewarded with expulsion from their party.

The great political divide hardened when the easy-going Baldwin gave way to the sharp and efficient Chamberlain; like Baldwin the new Prime Minister belonged to that business class which had risen to eminence on the wave of Victorian economic expansion: it was still very powerful – and when the young Foreign Secretary, Anthony Eden, resigned early in 1938, he was replaced by another (albeit ennobled) of its representatives, Lord Halifax. But though still powerful, this class was now out of touch with the essence of the society over which it ruled. Chamberlain's most recent biographer (Mr Iain Macleod) quotes his longing for the age 'before the days of motors and telephones' and his obscurantist opinion of the art of Stanley Spencer:

It rouses me to fury to think that . . . any otherwise intelligent person should be fool enough to try to admire it.

The change of Prime Ministers came just when Hitler was embarking upon the last stage of his designs upon Europe. In March, 1938, Austria was swallowed up, too quickly for the British to take any action. Czechoslovakia was clearly the next target. War seemed inevitable in September, 1938, with Britain and France apparently prepared to stand by the Czechs; but a series of hectic negotiations between Chamberlain and Hitler, culminating in the Munich settlement, postponed this prospect, though at the expense of reducing Czechoslovakia to a defenceless remnant.

Materially Britain gained little if anything from this postponement; but after Munich came the moment of truth: when Hitler proceeded to gobble up the remnant, no one in Britain or in the British Empire could any longer doubt the insatiability of his demands. When the invasion of Poland came in September, 1939, the country was ready, morally, to fight.

Mr Macleod and Mr A. J. P. Taylor (in his *Origins of the Second World War*) have recently attempted to pull the tablecloth away (in rather different directions) from under the carefully laid and long accepted interpretation of the events with which Chamberlain, primarily, was associated. We can salute the breakage of one or two quite ridiculous pieces of historical crockery, but on the whole the record in regard to the British Prime Minister has not been much altered. Clearly the policy of appeasement, that is to say, the constructive pursuit of peace, is the highest aim of diplomacy. It was an aim shared by Lloyd George, by the planners, by the League of Nations Union (a much traduced body, however: it did resolve in June, 1938, that any aggression upon Czechoslovakia should be regarded as an unfriendly act against Britain), and by the *New Statesman* and men of the left when they repeated time and again that Germany's 'legitimate grievances' must be met.

Too much emphasis should not be placed upon Chamberlain: at Munich he did a business deal with Hitler of which many of his fellow countrymen were thoroughly ashamed, but for which many others were profoundly thankful. Chamberlain was not unique. In the wider view Britain's involvement in a Second World War was due to a failure in consistency in her foreign policy since the end of the previous war. She was too idealistic to pursue a policy of repression towards Germany; she was too lacking in faith to give consistent support to the League of Nations where, alone, idealism could be made a positive force for peace.

The opening of the new war was in a sense part of the fabric of history that we have been discussing: a fabric in which the main threads have been the dreadful bleeding of potential political talent in the first war; the revulsion against strong political leadership; anti-militarism and the confusion of idealisms in foreign policy; the debilitating effects of continuous economic depression, and, in particular, the rousing of a social conscience at the expense of an internationalist mind; the estrangement from Government of the committed generation, guardians of the country's brains and courage; and, finally, the predominance in the political and social scene of a class which thought too readily in terms of the business deal.

PHASE IV : EXPLOSION, 1940-50

CHAPTER ELEVEN

THE FEVERED FORTIES

BRITAIN entered her second world war against Germany on 3rd September, 1939. Although this war, too, had explosive effects upon the development of British society, it did not hit the country with anything like the shock of the earlier war. Events in Manchuria, Abyssinia, and Spain had shown just what brutalities might be expected. In the event the air menace proved to be less than had been expected. ('The bomber always gets through', Baldwin, in one of his flesh-creeping moments, had predicted.) Over all, 300,000 British combatants were killed, while the civilian population suffered to the extent of 60,000 killed. In the Merchant Navy 30,000 men were lost. The theory and practice of total war was developed to a much fuller extent than in 1914–18. Provision for military conscription was actually made before the outbreak of war; and by its end five million men were in arms. Science, finally, was now of crucial importance.

Although the military controversies arising from the war occupy the usual extensive literature (there are no more prolific controversialists than unemployed generals), these are not of the same fundamental, and therefore socially important, nature as those arising from the First World War. For this reason only the barest outline will be given here of the course of this war (really better regarded as two wars – one against the Axis Powers, Germany and Italy, the other against Japan). We shall then proceed to a general assessment of the consequences of the war for British society.

The first autumn, winter, and spring of the war was fought under the shadow of the pact concluded at the very last moment between Russia and Germany; this phase is usually termed the 'phoney war', for there was little direct contact between the opposing nations. There was one interesting British success: the Germans had sown the British harbour approaches with magnetic mines – a device whose ingenuity, of course, was that the approaching ship summoned upon itself its own destruction. However an effective defence, the 'degaussing' girdle, was quickly produced by the scientists.

The pace hotted up with the German invasion of Scandinavia in April, 1940. It was the apparent completeness of the German success here which brought about the replacement of Chamberlain by Churchill (10th May). German successes continued with rapid advances both in East Europe and in the West, the latter culminating in the fall of France; Britain's one achievement was the skilful and courageous evacuation of Dunkirk. Now, with France under German domination, came Britain's first great crisis. This was the German attempt to open wide the way to total conquest by destroying the British Air Force: on 8th August the Battle of Britain began. Of the reasons usually given for the failure of the German attempt, perhaps three are of crucial importance. First of all the simple human factor, the superiority man for man of the British fighter pilots, the 'few' whose exploits have been so often hymned that they eventually became, in the revue, *Beyond the Fringe*, a target for satire. Second, the slight technical advantage of the Spitfire over the Messerschmidt; and third, the first exploitation of a new scientific development: radar (to give it its later and widely used name). It was in the months following the Battle of Britain that the roll of civilian victims to German bomber attacks reached the proportions that gave the country a unity in face of common danger not known in the First World War. The Government had already undertaken the large-scale evacuation of the country's mothers and children from the danger areas; although there were doubtless many incidents and irritations, the main consequence again was to stress the inter-dependence of the community. A general civilian black-out had been imposed since September, 1939; Air Raid Precautions did not meet with the same resentment as in the First World War.

The Battle of Britain was quickly fought and won; the other great death struggle, the Battle of the Atlantic, spread over several years, reaching its worst stages in 1942. The final achievement in keeping open the nation's food lines was a vital one. The next event on the world stage concerned Britain in ultimate consequence (and this was tremendous) rather than in immediate effect. Hitler began his invasion of Russia in June, 1941; just over a year later came one of the great turning-points in the war when after the successful defence of Stalingrad, the Russians began their own counter-offensive. Another world power had been brought into the war at the end of 1941; but not till 1943 did the Americans begin to get the Japanese, their main adversaries, on to the defensive.

Meanwhile the main land campaign involving British troops was being fought in North Africa, culminating, after a long and anxious ebb and flow of victory and defeat (the capture of Tobruk by the German General Rommel in June, 1942, at the time, seemed a disaster), in the Anglo-American invasion of Italy in July, 1943. The invasion of Normandy, the last phase of the war against Germany, and the one which brought her final surrender in early May, 1945, did not begin till the June of the previous year. There remained the final offensives against the Japanese in Burma and the Pacific; here the truly horrendous nature of scientific warfare was to reveal itself. On August 6th and August 8th, 1945, atomic bombs were dropped, on Hiroshima and Nagasaki. The Japanese surrender followed at once.

Now to the wider social consequences of the war. First of all, in an oft-quoted phrase of Sir Winston Churchill's, it made the trade unions an estate of the realm. This came about through the need to enlist the wholehearted support of the trade union movement in the country's war effort. It was signalized by the inclusion of Ernest Bevin, hitherto not even an M.P., as Minister of Labour in Churchill's War Coalition. At the end of the war the trade union movement had achieved its highest ever membership of over eight millions, and trade unionists were successfully voicing their claims to make direct representations to Government departments on any issue on which they felt themselves to be affected.

It might, however, be more significantly maintained that the war made science an estate of the realm, though this fact is still partially concealed because scientists are usually even less articulate than the dullest trade unionists.

Rutherford and his group continued their work on nuclear physics until Rutherford's death just before the war. At the outbreak of war the pace flagged as attention was directed to what were held to be more important projects. But from 1940 a new impetus was provided by the flight to England of Halban and Kowarski, two colleagues of the great French nuclear scientist, Joliot-Curie. Though Britain now established a lead in the preliminary development of atomic power, from 1942 all efforts were concentrated in North America, and the United States, assisted by British scientists, gained a monopoly in the production of the atomic bomb. Against this horror of horrors can be placed the exploitation for the first time of Alexander Fleming's neglected discovery (actually made in 1928) of penicillin: so intensive was the search for containers in which to grow the penicillin mould that yet another war-time problem was created – a shortage of milk bottles! After the war the commercial exploitation of penicillin and the other antibiotics was to add force to the industrial trend already discussed in connexion with the sulpha-drugs.

We have noted the vital defensive role in war of radar – the product, basically, of the researches of E. V. Appleton and R. H. Watson Watt: it was, in peace, equally indispensable for the safe passage of merchant shipping and civil aviation. Air travel, indeed, came of age during the Second World War. A century which had opened gaping wonderingly into the exhaust of the first motor-cars, was moving towards the jet age. Two other developments which are much in the public eye at the moment were stimulated by the war. The need to *miniaturize* produced the transistor radio; the need to compute at great speed the range and trajectories of rockets and shells produced the electronic computer, or 'adding machine'.

There was something of an interaction between the arts and sciences: artists like Julian Trevelyan and Bill Hayter, for example, were employed in the new technique of camouflage. In monetary terms the expansion of science is clear: in 1937 the country's total expenditure on science was £7·5 millions; in 1955 the figure was £315 millions (including, however, £214 millions of purely military expenditure).

More important, science was now a vital concern of Government. There was some recognition of this in the general allocation to the Lord President of the Council of the duties of a Minister of Science, and in the creation of a Cabinet Scientific Advisory Committee under the Chairmanship of professional scientist, F. A. Lindemann, created Lord Cherwell in 1942. It is here that the lack of any efficient integration of science into the framework of democratic decision-making reveals itself as a serious restraint upon the efficiency of Government itself. Cherwell was in fact a personal favourite of Churchill's; he was, as it were, the 'court scientist', and his greatest rival, Sir Henry Tizard, was effectively excluded from the counsels of the Government. It was Cherwell who instigated the policy of intensive bombing of the main German centres of population; it is now clear that the calculations upon which Cherwell based this policy were gravely inaccurate, and he has been held responsible by Sir Charles Snow (see his *Science and Government*) and others for a misuse of the country's resources in time of war (though Cherwell has been defended by the Earl of Birkenhead in his official biography, *The Prof in Two Worlds*). The basic point for us is the vital importance to Government of sound scientific advice; the dropping of two atom bombs merely rammed this home.

We have paid sufficient attention to cultural trends since 1914 to be aware that neither British Governments nor the British people were enthusiastic sponsors of artistic enterprises. Yet it seems clear that during the war the arts came to represent in a very real sense something that the British felt they were defending against Nazi tyranny and obscurantism: thus we have the founding of the Council for the

Encouragement of Music and the Arts, the forerunner of our present-day Arts Council. In his autobiography, *Indigo Days,* Julian Trevelyan has commented also that,

Wartime fellow feeling among painters accounts for the more tolerant and catholic acceptance of various styles that has come about since.

The most important novels of the time drew their subject matter from (in the case of J. B. Priestley), or set their scenes in (in the case of Graham Greene), the home front rather than the fields of battle. This in itself reflected significant change of climate between first war and second. But for the ordinary men who fought it, was this war much different from the first? If there was perhaps less passionate dedication there was probably a greater feeling of inescapable purpose: war resistance was a negligible factor this time. There was one important new feature of army life, and that was the emphasis throughout the services upon education. It was this that gave hope for a broader base for democratic development and cultural innovation after the war. It does indeed seem that in some perverse way wars turn men's minds to the question of the realization of their own potential. As a great historian of education has commented, 'It is not without significance that the Education Acts of 1870, 1902, 1918, 1944 were passed in time of war.' (Barnard, *History of English Education.*) Certainly the problems of evacuating children and incorporating them in new communities served to focus attention on their educational needs. With the 1914 Act we shall deal in the next chapter.

Wars also provoke a sense of national unity, often of a deplorable rabble-rousing type. But there is another kind. Here is an extract from the 1944 White Paper on Social Insurance, which, better than any further commentary, pins down the significance of the Second World War in British social history:

... the scheme as a whole will embrace, not certain occupations and income groups, but the entire population. Concrete expression is thus given to the solidarity and unity of the nation, which in war have been its bulwarks against aggression and in peace will be its guarantees of success against individual want and mischance.

Likewise another White Paper of the same year laid it down that any future Government would have as a major economic aim the maintenance of full employment.

Once again, in fact, the most important effect of the war was to speed up the trend towards collectivism; and collectivism, in the form of nationalization and socialization, continued to be a basic tenet of Government to the end of the forties. Indeed the decade 1940 to 1950 in many respects forms an economic unity, and will here be treated as such. The enforced imposition of controls in wartime created a not unfavourable climate for their retention by the post-war Labour Government, which, as it were, had them ready to hand. Furthermore many of the external problems of wartime continued long into the peace. In rough terms the overall process was this: the war created a number of major economic problems which the Government had to deal with at once; the solutions adopted in turn created a pile-up of serious problems at the end of the war which now had to be attacked by the post-war Labour Government. Hence the picture of feverish activity presented by the forties; not all of it, of course, necessary or salutary.

The basic problem of modern total war is to maximize the war effort at the expense of everything else. Two shortages had to be faced at once, that of manpower and that of food – especially serious during the anxious months of the Battle of the Atlantic. At the beginning of the war the unemployment level still stood at over a million, but by the end of 1940 a grave shortage in the engineering industry of the skilled men required by the new developments in mechanized warfare, became apparent. An immediate solution was found in schemes for the upgrading and training of labour and the pooling of key men. By mid-1942 the number of skilled men in the engineering trade had doubled, but even so the country was now in the midst of a widespread manpower crisis which extended from engineering to agriculture and chemicals (there was, of course, at the same time a constant expansion of the armed forces).

In face of this crisis the Government adopted two expedients: all other industries were ruthlessly cut back, and direction of manpower was introduced. To curtail the luxury, furniture, and clothing trades, utility standards were instituted. Petrol disappeared from the private market in 1942; and the coal industry, chronically ailing in the inter-war years, was now left to run down. From the outset the Minister of Labour had been provided with powers to direct

any person in the United Kingdom to perform any service required in any place. He might prescribe the remuneration of such services and the hours of work. He might require such persons to register particulars of themselves; he might order employers to keep and produce any records and books.

To such lengths did State power reach under the impact of the war. But in a country which had long been wont to conjure up the spectre of Bolshevist 'Nationalization of Women' the next step was even more astounding. In 1941 provision was made for the conscription of women between the ages of 20 and 30. Since most women have more fundamental things to do at this stage in their lives, the age range had, by 1943, been changed to 18½ to 50.

This colossal programme of direction and expansion of labour attained some remarkable achievements. The agricultural labour force stood at 711,000 in 1939; by 1945 it had been expanded to 887,000. In 1939 the engineering and chemical industries together employed 3·1 millions; in 1945 they employed 5·2 millions. And this took place at the same time as the armed forces expanded from 480,000 in 1939 to 5·1 millions in 1945. From producing 2,000 aircraft in 1939, the country from 1942 onwards was able to produce 8,000 to 12,000 a year. Similarly the production of tanks had gone up fourfold in 1942 as over 1940.

The food shortage was met by the direction and encouragement of farmers, through the use of subsidies – for ploughing in particular; livestock farming, which used up the country's resources at an uneconomical rate, on the other hand, was discouraged. British agriculture now for the first time became thoroughly mechanized, the number of tractors in use, for instance, leapt from 60,000 to 190,000. Like the manual worker the farmer achieved a new prosperity which he was not to shed when the war ended.

From the experience of the First World War the politicians had learned to beware of two things above all: inflation and profiteering. Just as the war brought Winston Churchill from the wilderness, it did the same for J. M. Keynes, who after joining the Treasury in 1940 was able to lay a strong hand on Government economic policy. To ensure fair shares of limited resources the Government instituted a system of rationing by coupons and 'points'. (Of the latter economists were particularly proud, because it maintained some sort of limited freedom of choice.) To reinforce these systems against the price inflation which had vitiated the attempts at fair shares in the first war, food subsidies were introduced in 1940; from £72 millions in that year they rose to £215 millions in 1944. Excess income was mopped up through the boosting of the National Savings Campaign, and through heavy taxation: levied at 60 per cent in 1939, the Excess Profits Tax rose to 100 per cent in 1940; the standard rate of income tax reached ten shillings in 1940, and there were pretty crippling duties on beer, spirits and tobaccos.

This high level of taxation played its part in solving another fundamental problem of the war: how was it to be financed? It says something for the country's stewardship that only half of the burden was placed on posterity as opposed to the two-thirds of the 1914–18 war. For the necessary ready cash Britain had to turn to her overseas assets. By March, 1941, her dollar resources were drained practically dry; fortunately the United States came to her aid at this point with the Lend-Lease Agreements, which were a mixture of friendly generosity and hard business acumen. (In the general settlement of accounts at the end of the war, it should be said, American generosity prevailed.) In 1939 Britain had overseas assets of £3,000 millions; in the course of the war she used up over a third of these. Of her initial gold reserves of £450 millions she spent two-thirds on the war. And to complete the gloomy picture, she had, by 1945, increased her external debt by £3,000 millions.

Here in part is the clue to the chronic balance of payments crises which were to afflict the country in the years following the war. Perhaps even more serious was the fact that in concentrating on her war effort Britain had lost two-thirds of her world markets; practically her whole South American market, so important since the days of Castlereagh and Canning, for example, was lost to the United States. Nor was the domestic economy left in a particularly fine state to meet the new challenge. The railways and the basic industries had, necessarily, been flogged almost to death. Enforced neglect and enemy action induced a serious building shortage, particularly desperate in housing and in the shipyards.

On the other hand under the impact of war the nation had undergone a massive extension of its collectivist machinery, and – as we have seen – a substantial development in its economic and social ideology. These changes, of course, were entirely in line with the ideas, springing from the late nineteenth century but first set in vigorous action by the Great War, left rather at a discount in the twenties, and canvassed again by the most brilliant members of the community in the thirties. At the centre of government the exigencies of war undoubtedly produced a bureaucratization too great to be borne in time of peace. The following new ministries were established: in 1939, the Ministry of Supply; in 1940, the Ministries of Home Security, Economic Welfare, Information, Food, Shipping, and Aircraft Production. The new social ideology was given striking expression in the report presented in December, 1942, by the distinguished civil servant, Sir William (later Lord) Beveridge, embracing the findings of an inquiry he had conducted into the social services, in which he advocated a unified structure covering the entire community; and later in the two White Papers of 1944 to which we have referred.

Most politicians were prepared to accept the necessity for

further steps in social reform; the Labour party accorded the sweeping Beveridge proposals a particularly enthusiastic reception. Thus at the end of the war whatever Government came to power would be faced with three rather contrary objectives. On the one hand it was committed to the extension of the social services, a policy necessarily involving a high level of taxation and a tendency towards inflation. On the other hand it had to fight the balance of payments crisis by, at all costs, increasing exports, a policy which could be successful only if British prices were kept down and the community accepted a discipline antithetical to the developments in welfare legislation. Finally there would have to be intensive investment to revive the failing domestic industries; this policy, too, would necessitate a spirit of self-sacrifice on the part of the war-weary community, and might also involve a conflict of priorities with the export drive.

To reconcile the conflicts, the theorizing of the thirties and the practical experience of the recent war would have to be exploited to the full: there would have to be a very careful planning of the country's resources. Perhaps the country sensed this, returning to office the party which committed itself most clearly to the concept of the planned economy. Not, however, that the Labour party's attachment to economic planning was entirely based upon a realistic appraisal of the problems facing the community: it was in large part ideological, stemming from a belief that an equalitarian society could only be based upon the common ownership (which came in effect to mean State ownership) of the main means of production, distribution and exchange.

Immediately upon taking office the Labour Government was faced with the American decision to bring the Lend-Lease Agreements to an abrupt end. Their replacement by a generous £1,000 million dollar loan enabled the Government to weather the crisis. The extent to which the British economy was being bolstered by the Americans became a ready coin in the bitter exchanges of domestic politics, and a source of uneasiness and ungraciousness on the part of both right and left. The Conservative weekly, the *Economist*, put the matter patriotically but not unfairly:

Our present needs are the direct consequences of the fact that we fought earliest, that we fought longest, and that we fought hardest. In moral terms we are creditors.

Balance of payments crises became an endemic feature of the British economy, while one final economic difficulty came with the assumption, in the light of the post-war international situation, of the heavy burden of rearmament.

The Government proceeded towards its objective of a planned economy based on communal ownership by the following stages: in 1946 the Bank of England was nationalized; in 1947 the Coal Mines (by this time in a deplorable state) followed, as, in 1948, did the Supply of Electricity, the Railways (also in poor condition) and Road Transport, although part of the original programme, the nationalization of the Iron and Steel Industry, had to be postponed because of the resistance of the Conservative majority in the House of Lords. Throughout, a strict policy of controls, quotas, and the bulk purchase of imports was maintained.

Keynesian dogma was now a political commonplace. Hugh Dalton, Chancellor of the Exchequer in the first years of the Labour Government, followed a deliberate cheap money policy, with the Bank Rate at the low figure of 2 per cent. The Government was especially concerned that the wartime pledges to create a full employment society should be observed. The maintenance of full employment, in which the bargaining position of the trades unions, naturally, is at its strongest, inevitably creates an inflationary pressure. The Government was far from successful in its efforts to combat this, though it could with total justice argue that the greater good far outweighed the lesser evil.

In 1947, in endeavouring to fulfil its promise to the United States to restore the convertibility of sterling, the Government precipitated a desperate economic crisis, which roused legitimate doubts as to the competence of its management of the country's resources. However, the austere policies of Dalton's successor, Sir Stafford Cripps, slowly pulled the nation to safety. Cripps attempted to meet the inflationary danger by bringing the trades unions into co-operation with the Government in a policy of wage restraint, a solid recognition of their new status in the community. A short-term fillip to exports was given by the devaluation of the pound in 1949.

On the whole the economy of the country made a fair ascent from the chaotic depths of 1945. Taking 1938 as 100, the figures for exports are: 1945, 45·8; 1946, 99·3; 1947, 108·8; 1948, 136·3; 1949, 150; and 1950, 175. And the country at the same time completed its social revolution. To that we now turn.

CHAPTER TWELVE

THE SOCIAL REVOLUTION

CAN one legitimately speak of a 'social revolution' in Britain in the 1940's? For one thing it cannot be said that nationalization did much, as Socialists had once believed it would do, to further social equality: the men at the top remained the same, and the ordinary workman had little sense of 'communal' ownership. For another thing the emergence of a fully developed welfare state was in a sense merely the logical conclusion to a process which we have been studying since its early (but not original) phases around 1914. What justifies the adjective 'revolutionary' is, first, the total comprehensiveness of the new welfare schemes, and, second, the striking changes in social behaviour in the community at large.

We have already noted the sense of unity fostered by the war which created the right climate for the comprehensive social insurance outlined in the 1944 White Paper. We have also noted the impetus given to science; and this had the interesting side effect of turning scientific minds to the problems of public health and social security. The existing social services, due to their piecemeal growth, were full of gaps and anomalies. Apart from all other considerations it was clearly in the interests of efficiency that the new social services should be consolidated and comprehensive. The editor of *Social Security*, published in 1943, expressed the scientific outlook:

... if persons with qualified and trained minds will apply themselves in a disinterested manner to a great social problem of this kind, the proper principles will emerge so unmistakably that the right solution will cease to be a matter of mere opinion and become a question of scientific knowledge.

Lastly, the post-war system owed its all-embracing character to the ideological aversion of the political party responsible (as it happened) for bringing it into being, to any hint of class distinction or social snobbery such as would be implied in schemes restricted to the 'working class'.

Let us look at the actual construction of the Welfare State. The solid rock beneath was full employment. The first pillars were the conversion in 1940 of the old Unemployment Assistance Board into a National Assistance Board, and the decree of 1941 that family resources were no longer to be taken into consideration when assessing the merits of a claim for Assistance. As Ernest Bevin commented:

the only thing now left of Queen Elisabeth was one toe sticking out of the ground and that for the rest the Poor Law was now buried.

The key plan upon which all subsequent building was based was the Beveridge Report of 1942. One of Beveridge's most important recommendations was implemented by the war Coalition in the Family Allowances Act of 1945.

The insurance side of the structure was completed by two acts of 1946 and two of 1948, and the establishment in the latter year of a separate Ministry of National Insurance. The parent act of 1946 swept together the untidy litter of existing legislation and swept away the Lloyd George system of farming out to private insurance societies. The State assumed responsibility for more than half of the total cost of the scheme, the remainder being met by a poll tax upon employee and employer.

The free National Health Service, the pride of the whole edifice, was brought into existence by the National Health Service Act of 1946, ratified only after the bitter opposition of much of the medical profession had been overcome. Other snags were quickly encountered: doctors, nurses, and administrators were in short supply. Governmental emphasis on maintaining the country's full employment capacity meant that hospital building lagged far behind factory building. In order that the problems of the future might be promptly dealt with as they arose, the Minister of Health (Aneurin Bevan) was given very wide paper powers; this augmentation in central authority, reasonable enough in intention, roused much concern. However the Health Service quickly established itself: in 1950, 95 per cent of the population of 50 millions was making use of it; and it embraced 90 to 95 per cent of the country's general practitioners, 90 per cent of the dentists, and nearly 100 per cent of the pharmacists.

Malnutrition, we have seen, was still a rampant evil in the thirties. A cheap and plentiful supply of basic foods was as essential to the wellbeing of the community as free medical services. Food subsidies, originally introduced in 1940 on a modest scale, were expanded by both wartime and post-war Governments; by 1948 they were costing the exchequer £485 millions per annum. The wartime distribution of free or heavily subsidised welfare foods to children and expectant mothers, was expanded. In 1948 about 98 per cent of the country's school children were each drinking one third of a pint of free milk daily.

As the bombs began to fall in 1940 and century-old slums tottered to the ground, many theories were advanced on the future reconstruction of our towns and villages. Thus was Town and Country Planning, so long so tentatively approached, conceived on a truly national scale. By an Act of 1944 subsidies could be granted to local planning authorities. In 1946 came the imaginative New Towns Act which quickly bore fruit in the sparkling (though, some said, soulless) new towns at Harlow, Glenrothes, and other places, particularly on the periphery of London and in the Lowlands of Scotland. The 1947 Town and Country Planning Act, the consequence of the deliberations of the Uthwatt Committee, was revolutionary in its attempt to deal with the planner's great bugbear, the cost of land. The old Socialist nostrum of land nationalization, the Committee said, in practice offered too many complications: the Government therefore took the step of nationalizing, not the land itself, but the development rights in it. The Act, further, gave encouragement to the local planning authorities to survey their own planning needs; it gave them valuable powers in the matter of the preservation of historic buildings and of woodlands, and in the restraint of outdoor advertising. One of the great symbols of the social revolution was the

National Parks and Access to the Countryside Act of 1949; here, in the setting aside of large tracts of the countryside as National Parks, was the first major attempt to reverse the spoliation of the country's natural beauty which had been in course since the early industrial revolution.

The Labour Government was far from successful in meeting the country's gigantic housing problem. The 1946 and 1949 Housing Acts continued and extended the policy of subsidized local authority housing, but inadequate living accommodation continued to be one of the most grievous burdens borne by the community. The latter Act, again, is of great symbolic importance in that for the first time in a Housing Act the phrase 'working class' is omitted – the emphasis once again is on comprehensiveness, on the unity of the community rather than on its fragmentation into classes.

We have seen something of the impact of war upon education. Two parallel developments, which coalesced in the 1944 Education Act, took place during the war. On the one hand attention was given to the overall question of educational policy: first thoughts appeared in the 'Green Book' of 1941, published, as was wryly remarked at the time, 'in a blaze of secrecy'. The results of the further deliberations of the responsible ministers, R. A. Butler and Chuter Ede, emerged in July, 1943, in the White Paper, *Educational Reconstruction*. On the other hand a series of Committees thrashed out specific educational problems. Thus the Fleming Committee dealt with the relationship of the public schools to the educational system, the McNair Committee with the problem of the recruitment and training of teachers, and the Norwood Committee with the question of university entrance.

The 1944 Act conceived of education as being organized in three progressive stages: primary, secondary, and further education (the old notion of 'elementary' education, never fully eradicated, now went for good). Responsibility for the provision of primary and secondary education was placed firmly on the local authorities, who were, in addition, to make available scholarships and grants for further education. The local authorities, finally, were to provide nursery schools and special schools. The school-leaving age was, without exception, to be fifteen (the expressed hope that it would be raised at a later date to sixteen, proved, as Randolph Hearst said in another connexion, to be like winking at a girl in the dark – well-intentioned, but ineffective).

As defined by the Act the country's education was, in essence, left in the hands of four main types of school. Most numerous were the free 'County' schools; also free were the 'Voluntary' schools, substantially assisted by the local authority but catering for such special groups in the community as, for example, the Roman Catholics. Third came the 'Direct Grant' schools, so called because their outside aid (additional to their revenue from fees) came direct from the State rather than from the local authority – the difference is more apparent than real, and is little more than a piece of empty snobbism: these fee-paying schools comprised most of the better grammar schools in England and the old-established day schools in Scotland. Fourthly there remained, outside the general framework, the various types of Private school which did now, however, have to conform to certain basic standards.

It was hoped that a recognition of the needs of the modern world would be found in the division of the secondary stage of education between grammar schools of the old type, and 'modern' schools with a definite technological orientation. The transition from primary to secondary was marked by an examination taken at the age of 'eleven plus', upon the results of which the child's future at either a grammar or a modern school was to be determined. In theory grammar and modern schools were to be regarded as equal, but since in practice this parity was never achieved, there was much criticism of the policy of child segregation on the basis of an examination taken at an immature age ('The rat race begins at eleven plus', as the *New Statesman* later put it). It was also argued that the preservation of Direct Grant and Private schools was out of keeping with the egalitarian society which the social revolution otherwise came near to creating.

As with the National Health Service, the biggest obstacles

to a full implementation of the new educational policy were physical. For a start there was a crying need for 70,000 new teachers and 600,000 new school places. When finally the leaving age was raised to fifteen in 1947 neither gap had been plugged. Although the parent Act dealt explicitly with the question of teachers' salaries and removed such quaint Victoriana as the bar, in force in some areas, upon the employment of married women, it remained a fact that the State was unprepared to recognize in monetary terms the vital service rendered to the community by the teaching profession. Thus it happened that for all the idealism of the 1944 Act, a large section of the community continued to receive a second-rate education in overcrowded fourth-rate surroundings. Still, a rise in the general level of education, and the theoretical opportunity (often circumscribed in practice by family circumstances and attitudes) for higher education for all, were factors of overwhelming importance in the new trends of social behaviour.

What were the consequences of the revolution? The high cost of the social services, involving a fourfold increase in taxation between 1938 and 1949, of itself meant a considerable redistribution of income. In 1938 7,000 people had incomes of over £6,000 per annum after taxation; in 1947–48 the comparable figure was 70. None the less even in the grim austerity of 1945–50 it was clear that a number of people were managing to do very well for themselves, exploiting the Inland Revenue's tolerance of expense accounts and the absence of any taxation of capital gains, and honouring the five-shilling limit imposed upon restaurant meals only in the breach. It might therefore be argued that relatively speaking it was the professional middle class which suffered most from the changes. Yet it was in fact the middle-income group which made greatest use of such of the new social services as higher education, which in many cases the less well off were simply not in a position to make use of.

For the community as a whole the most stunning changes were in health and wellbeing, in which qualities this country left even prosperous America behind. In the last of his three social surveys of York, Seebohm Rowntree discovered that

post-war children in all sections of the community were taller
and heavier than in 1936. In 1950 infant mortality fell below
thirty per thousand for the first time in British history. Even
the birthrate began to show an upward movement, the first
reversal of the trend of three-quarters of a century, apart from
the brief baby boom of 1920.

Did all this mean that the Briton was now cocooned in
cotton wool from the cradle to the grave? Fears were expressed that his moral fibre was being endangered. The
evidence hardly warrants any such conclusion. From 1945 to
1950, as we have noted, it was only the great gains in total
output which enabled the country to survive her balance of
payments crises. On *a priori* grounds it is arguable that it is
when basic needs are satisfied, basic fears are met, and a decent
standard of leisure and comfort established, that a community
is best able to attain its highest cultural potential.

The community was better educated than ever before (the
Education Corps had attempted to do for adults what was now
being done for children): it had a greater sense of social
security than ever before; and it had money to spend. This,
of course, is putting things at their brightest. It had also to
put up with the maintenance of wartime restrictions and
rationing, frequent crises and shortages. It had to put up with
the greatest culinary curiosity since shepherd's pie, Snoek; it
had to put up with petty bureaucracy ('snoopers'), real or
imagined, and it had to put up with spivvery and black market-
eering, particularly in commodities such as nylons, which
would have added a touch of glamour to life. If there was
optimism in post-1945 Britain, there was also a certain Cal-
vinistic greyness.

But the diffusion of education, the security, the money are
positive factors in the post-war cultural developments. Unhappily the equation is only completed by a fourth factor: the
great technological advances in mass communication. Thus
between 1945 and 1950 there is an absolute increase in the
amount of entertainment, in the broadest sense, absorbed by
the community. What development there is in truly vital
cultural activity is more difficult to define.

Where quantitative increase was most marked was in reading. Between 1937 and 1947 the total circulation of national and provincial daily newspapers increased by fifty per cent, so that at the latter date each household on average was taking roughly two newspapers. In the same period the total circulation of Sunday newspapers doubled, while from sales of twenty-six millions in 1938, magazines and periodicals reached a sale of over forty millions by 1952. Advertising, we have seen, dominated many of the earlier newspaper trends; this would be less true of the period up to 1950, when, with a persistent shortage of newsprint and, consequently, rather small newspapers, advertisers were begging for space.

After 1945 the threefold division of newspapers by type hardened perceptibly. The majority group based itself on the vast new reading public created by the educational changes of the war. Beaverbrook's *Express*, brilliantly edited by Arthur Christiansen, politically negligible despite the loud insistence of his master's voice, was of the utmost significance in fostering a climate of snobbism and economic one-upmanship. The *Mirror*, placed on the circulation throne by the war (every serviceman appreciated its pin-ups), preserved its thirtyish sense of social purpose throughout the forties, but in the main concentrated on the sensational and the trivial. An exceptional circulation, based on its spinsterish reportage of the shabbier court cases, was maintained by the Sunday *News of the World*, rightly described by Francis Williams (in his *Dangerous Estate*) as the most traditional of all newspapers; its circulation was not, however, rising, as was the case with the *Mirror*, the *Express*, the *Mail* and the other populars.

Rising circulation was also reported by papers of a very different type: *The Times*, the *Telegraph*, the *Manchester Guardian*, the *Sunday Times* and the *Observer*, 'quality' papers appealing to a limited, but, clearly, expanding circle. Only one type of paper was having a hard time of it: that which tried to establish a balance between being popular and being quality; thus the *News Chronicle* was already having a difficult job in making ends meet. The division, in fact, was hardening into a twofold one. It seemed that in the contemporary newspaper world there was to be as sharp a distinction between the classes and the masses as ever there was in the Victorian social world.

That the position of the Press was a matter of concern in political circles can be seen from the appointment of a Royal Commission on the Press in 1946; this concern was heightened by the resumption after the war of the process whereby more and more newspaper power was concentrated in fewer and fewer hands. From its two-year labour the Royal Commission brought forth a mouse among mice, the Press Council – a body which, in the fifties, proved unable to exercise any control over the Press.

Book production was higher in Britain than in any other country. In 1950 a poll was conducted into personal reading habits. Fifty-five per cent of those interviewed claimed at the time of the poll to be reading a book. The reading matter was 'mostly fiction', but it is at least arguable that the imaginative demands made by all but the most trivial novels are far greater than those of the factual technological studies described as 'serious reading'.

The main trends concealed in this rather vague evidence have been the subject of some argument. It does seem clear that up to 1950 at any rate the divisions between mass and minority culture were again being accentuated, but that the minority culture itself was greatly extending its appeal. A race, an unequal one perhaps, but none the less a race, was well under way; while the forces of commercialism were redoubling their efforts to make the ordinary man accept unquestioningly the peelings of his rightful cultural heritage, he was also being given a far greater opportunity than ever before of enjoying its fruits.

There were many hopeful signs. Britain's music renaissance continued. By taking over the running of the Henry Wood Promenade Concerts the BBC made them available to a much wider public. In 1946 the Third Programme was established to provide a hearing for serious music (and for serious topics generally). The step, however, was not altogether a laudable one, since the new programme from the outset was the preserve of a very limited audience, and thus served to emphasise the exclusiveness of minority culture.

At the highest level Britain made a better showing on the cultural map than she had for a long time. With his opera *Peter Grimes*, Benjamin Britten emerged as one of the greatest of contemporary composers, while Margot Fonteyn established herself as one of the world's leading ballerinas. And the inauguration in 1947 of the Edinburgh Festival of Music and Drama, which marched on to undreamt-of successes, ranged the Scottish capital among the foremost cultural centres of the world.

Appreciation of painting appeared to be growing. Art sales did well, without there being (as in Victorian times) an obvious prostitution of art to the demands of the upper middle-class market. The great Van Gogh Exhibition of 1947 attracted 12,000 visitors per day to the Tate Gallery. The best British painting was essentially individualistic and unaffected by conformity to prevailing 'isms': it ranged through the flat, patterned landscapes of Ivon Hitchens, the intense romanticism of John Piper, to the bustling humanity of L. S. Lowry's Lancashire scenes. Scotland, aided by the tradition established by the 'Glasgow School' at the end of the previous century and continued by the great 'colourists', Peploe, Ferguson and Hunter, and by the fact that the Royal Scottish Academy, unlike its English counterpart, imposed no dead hand upon Scottish painting, was artistically particularly alive; the work of Anne Redpath, W. S. Gillies and many others suggested that many of the complaints about the centralization and standardization of culture were not well founded.

The first great post-war art controversy blew up in 1946 over the cleaning of old masters: the National Gallery and the *avant garde* claimed that the paintings were simply being relieved of the 'sweet treacly sauce' which was smothering them, while Sir Gerald Kelly and others declared that the paintings were being 'skinned alive'. An exhibition of the use of radiography in the examination and care of paintings gained a total attendance of 625,000. Once again the battalions of science had marched into the realms of the arts.

Yet concern was being expressed over a divide between the arts and sciences more serious in many respects than that between minority and mass culture. As industry called out for more and yet more men with a scientific or technological training, as it became more and more a fact of modern economic life that a science qualification would bring higher probable earnings than an equivalent arts qualification, the tendency towards the provision and acceptance of a quick and concentrated scientific education divorced from any grounding in the arts, increased. At the same time the increasing complications and ramifications of scientific knowledge put it further and further beyond the reach of the arts men. (One institution which, inspired by the genius of the political scientist, A. D. (Lord) Lindsay, sought to reverse the trend, was the new University College of North Staffordshire.) The division between what Sir Charles Snow was to term the 'two cultures' (a much used word, whose connotation varied very much according to its user), was, we have seen, particularly serious at Government level.

The social revolution had created a tremendous expansion in opportunity to lead the good life; but at the same time some of the problems militating against that life had increased in seriousness. In general the following decade, as we shall see in the next section of this book, was to bring an intensification of these problems.

CHAPTER THIRTEEN

POLITICS AND SOCIETY

WE have seen something of the bitter divide in the politics of the thirties, of the temptation to talk and even act in terms of extra-parliamentary violence. In the forties there comes a restoration of the more traditional situation in which two parties are firmly anchored in the calm waters of wide political agreement on basic issues. The elimination of the Liberals and the various Independents who stand outside the rigid two-party system continues. We find, too, the restoration of political leadership on a more heroic scale: Churchill and Attlee are neo-Victorians who can stand comparison with the great political leaders of the past. Churchill was never more wrong than when he described Attlee as 'a sheep in sheep's clothing'.

There could be no agreement whatsoever between Conservatives and Labour as long as Chamberlain remained in office. Though Churchill and Hankey were brought in, the Opposition refused to participate in the War Cabinet of nine which Chamberlain set up. The Government still seemed lacking in vigour, and discontent steadily mounted in Parliament, till it broke through upon the news of the evacuation of Norway. It was a Conservative, Amery, who, repeating Cromwell's address to the Long Parliament, made the most dramatic denunciation:

You have sat too long here for any good you have been doing. Depart, I say, and let us have done with you. In the name of God, go.

Chamberlain's attempt at defence was almost pitiable:

I do not seek to evade criticism but I say this to my friends in the House – and I have friends in the House . . . At least we

shall see who is with us and who is against us, and I call on my
friends to support us in the Lobby tonight.

It was left to Lloyd George to make the pertinent comment:

It is not a question of who are the Prime Minister's friends . . .
He has appealed for sacrifice. . . . I say solemnly that the Prime
Minister should give an example of sacrifice, because there is
nothing which can contribute more to victory in this war than
that he should sacrifice the seals of office.

The Government majority fell to eighty-one. Clearly change
was imperative, though Chamberlain still believed that he himself could survive. This belief foundered on continued Labour
hostility. The man the Opposition was prepared to serve under
was Churchill; thus on 10th May the Churchill Coalition took 1940
office. His first War Cabinet consisted of Churchill, Chamberlain, Halifax (neither yet discarded), Attlee and Greenwood.
One of Churchill's cleverest strokes was the appointment as
Minister of Labour of Ernest Bevin, who thus, overnight,
changed from a trade union boss into a political boss. At the
end of the year Bevin, along with Lord Beaverbrook, was
brought into the Cabinet; so, later, was Cripps, though he was
still an outcast from the Labour party. Other peripherally
political figures utilized by Churchill were Sir John Anderson,
the Hankey, as it were, of World War II, and Lord Woolton,
who as Minister of Food impinged more directly perhaps than
any other minister on the ordinary life of the people.

The only politician to serve with Churchill throughout the
entire length of the war was Attlee, given in 1941 the title of
Deputy Prime Minister. We have been left with an illuminat-
ing comparison between the Prime Minister and his Deputy:

When Attlee takes the chair, Cabinet meetings are businesslike
and efficient; we keep to the agenda, make decisions and get
away in reasonable time. When Mr Churchill presides nothing
is decided; we listen enthralled and go home, many hours late,
feeling that we have been present at an historic occasion.

How do we explain the phenomenon of Winston Churchill
in terms of social history? In the gay twenties and the committed thirties he had been an outsider; he had been a lone

thunderer in an era of pacifist idealism. But now, in guiding the fortunes of the country in a war into which it had stumbled backwards, he was in the job he, in his own words, 'liked the best'. The inter-war dream was over: what the country needed was some good nineteenth-century vigour; and this, transfigured by his own personal genius, Churchill admirably supplied. He asserted a far firmer political control over the British war effort than ever Lloyd George had succeeded in doing; he was himself a participant in military strategy and fertile in new military ideas. Added to this Churchill, with his great soaring cathedrals of sentences, buttressed by a breath-taking phraseology, provided a public leadership, unfashionable since the days of the Gothic revival, which in time of war provided the country with the inspiration it required.

Till the Summer of 1942 Churchill carried all before him in Parliament, save for three ILP M.P.s who formed the only true Opposition. Even the fall of Tobruk raised a mere twenty-five dissident votes. More serious was the growth of opposition on domestic issues. There was a widespread feeling that Churchill and his associates were too little aware of the social stirrings of the time, too hesitant on the question of implementing the Beveridge Report. Between 1942 and the end of the war, anti-Government candidates won eight by-elections and in the latter stages Sir Richard Acland founded his Commonwealth party since it was not possible for the Labour party to express open opposition to a Government of which it was itself a member. Inside Parliament, despite the official Labour attitude, there was in 1943 a hostile vote of 119 on the question of social security.

With the development of these disagreements on social policy, it is not surprising that the Coalition did not long survive the defeat of Germany. Labour left the Government, and a 'Caretaker' Ministry held office from 25th May, 1945, till the results of the general election, held on 5th July, were known. (This was not till the end of the month, because of the difficulty involved in counting the servicemen's votes.)

Consequent upon the social and economic changes we have already discussed, there were a number of distinctive features about this election. Mass communications played a bigger part than ever before. The broadcasting of speeches by the national political leaders, in particular, meant that the personality and quality of the individual candidates was of very secondary importance. Of the two major parties, Labour made much the more effective use of this important medium. Churchill rather lost touch, declaring of his opponents in his broadcast of 4th June, that 'they would have to fall back on some sort of Gestapo': the rhetoric which had helped to win the war was now helping to win the election – for Labour. In contrast, Attlee's calm and constructive speech of the following evening for the first time established him in the public eye (or the public ear, perhaps) as a first-rank politician. The new circulation giant, the *Daily Mirror*, too, threw its weight behind Labour, as, to be fair, did more selective publicists like Hulton of *Picture Post*.

If there were greater mass pressures than ever before, there was an electorate better educated, and therefore better able to resist them, than ever before. Windy speeches did not go down well with a public which looked rather for carefully factual policy statements. Here again, as it happened, Labour, which after all had had fifteen years in which to think, scored.

Without doubt the electorate looked back in anger to the hardships of the inter-war years, firmly associated in its mind with the Conservative party. But the election was not just fought on the record of the past. There was in 1945 a definite sense of hope in the future, well captured by J. B. Priestley in his short novel *Three Men in New Suits* (1945): Alan, Herbert, and Eddie, newly demobbed, had sprung from very different social environments, 'yet there was a distinct likeness between them, as if all three had come from the same place, and had been doing the same things there'; the peroration, on which all are agreed, is Alan's:

We don't want the same kind of men looking after our affairs. We act as if we've learnt something. We don't keep shouting 'That's mine – clear off!' We don't try to make our little corner safe – and to hell with anybody else! We don't talk about liberty when what we really mean is a chance to fleece the public. We don't go back on all we said when the country was in danger. We stop trying for some easy money. We do an honest job of work for the community for what the community thinks we're worth. We stop being lazy, stupid and callous. . . . Instead of guessing and grabbing, we plan. Instead of competing, we co-operate. We come out of the nursery – and begin to grow up!

4. Planning and radical social reform were indeed, as we have seen, in the air. Again the Labour party, on the evidence of its manifesto, *Let Us Face the Future*, alone, seemed most firmly committed to giving substance to these aspirations.

The result – Labour 393, Conservatives 213, Liberals 12, ILP 3, Communists 2, with 14 Independents – need not, then, be accounted a surprise. Although under Attlee's Prime Ministership the size of the Cabinet once again rose to twenty, some of the elements of wartime administrative techniques were maintained in the designation of four leading ministers, Morrison, Bevin, Cripps, and Alexander, as 'Co-ordinators', and in the extended use of Cabinet Committees. In so far as there was a Minister responsible for Science it was Morrison. The new 'court scientist' was Sir Henry Tizard, who although generally given a better Press than the man he replaced, Cherwell, has been criticized for giving insufficient encouragement to scientific research.

One of the first acts of the new Government was to restore the legal position of the trades unions to what it had been prior to the 1927 Trades Disputes Act; once again the political levy was to be based on 'contracting out' instead of 'contracting in'. Conservatives talked darkly of reversing this Act, but after a dozen years in office they have so far not attempted to do so. The Government's nationalization programme (see Chapter Eleven) was very hotly contested by the Opposition. By the time the Iron and Steel Nationalization Bill was produced in the Autumn of 1948 it was clear that it had little chance of reaching the statute book before the next general election, since the House of Lords (an overwhelmingly Conservative body) still had the power under the 1911 Act to delay measures for two years.

The Government, accordingly, had in the previous session

introduced a <u>Parliament Bill</u> designed to reduce <u>this delaying time to one year</u>. Again there was strong resistance, but after fruitless all-party discussions in February and May, 1948, the bill was duly enacted in 1949. Although, ironically, no resort to its provisions has yet been made, this measure can be regarded as a further stage in the democratization of British institutions. Despite the various proposals which emanated from the Conservative party nothing was done about the hereditary (and therefore clearly anti-democratic) character of the second chamber; the Labour Government shirked this issue, preferring to see the House of Lords a weakened anachronism rather than a revitalized force in the modern constitution. It remains to be said that the upper House played a valuable, even indispensable, part in sharing the extremely heavy legislative burden imposed on Parliament in the post-war years. One other detail in the democratization process was filled in: in 1948 the two remaining divagations from the principle of one man one vote, the business and university votes, were abolished.

The growth of collectivism, theoretically designed to further the essential economic and social freedom of the individual, may eventually begin to menace that very liberty. Ministerial powers were greatly increased during and after the war, centralization and bureaucracy infringed steadily upon the lives of everyone. But with the new dangers there came new safeguards. Two Parliamentary Committees, the Committee of Public Accounts, and the Committee on Estimates, helped to restrain ministers from exceeding the authority given to them by Parliament. The delegation of legislative details by an overworked Parliament to the Civil Service was denounced as long ago as 1929 by Lord Hewart, in his book *The New Despotism.* Again, however, a Committee on Statutory Instruments, established in 1944, provided a parliamentary check upon any piece of delegated legislation which appeared to go beyond the original general powers granted by Parliament.

In August, 1945, a Select Committee on Parliamentary Procedure was set up. Its *Third Report*, published in October, 1946, had this to say:

E

The danger to parliamentary government in this country at the present time is less likely to arise from lack of confidence in it than from the overwhelming burden which the growth of governmental activity places upon it. This burden has become greater, not less, with the arrival of peace, and it seems probable that it may increase. It is therefore a matter for constant vigilance to ensure that the machine is continuously adapted and strengthened to bear the new burdens put upon it.

The rationalization of parliamentary procedure took the form of greater use of smaller committees; thus less and less business appeared to be transacted across the actual floor of the House of Commons. To some observers Parliament seemed to be changing its character – hence the unflattering picture of its activities presented, for example, in the film *No Love for Johnnie*. In fact as long as the constitution retained its democratic base, increased efficiency at the top meant an increasingly efficient democracy.

Little has been said so far in this book of the British Empire and Commonwealth. The interaction between British democracy and the overseas territories acquired over the centuries by a fine mixture of naked aggression, commercial ambition, evangelical zeal, commonsense, hypocrisy, and sheer absence of mind, has proved worthy of many separate studies. Suffice it to say that the explosion of British society over the period 1914 to 1963 coincided with a radical change in the British Empire; in all but a few intractable segments, the British Empire became the British Commonwealth. Relationships with the white settlement colonies, Canada, Australia, New Zealand and South Africa (here, however, the problem was complicated by the Dutch ancestry of the major element of the white population, and, more critically, by the existence of a black native majority) were worked out in the inter-war years. With India, the great sub-continent which had since the eighteenth century loomed large in the fact and myth of British society, the final accounting was not achieved till after the war.

The Indian independence movement had been gathering strength since at least the beginning of the century. It was not without its sympathizers in this country: in the greatest of all his novels, *A Passage to India* (1924), E. M. Forster sympathetically explored its complications – the hostility between Moslem and Hindu, the subtle love-hate attitude towards the British – and the deplorable *de haut en bas* manner of the Anglo-Indian class; Ramsay MacDonald and Stanley Baldwin together laboured hard for Indian self-government – it was not their fault that the Government of India Act of 1935 never came fully into operation. But it was the Second World War which revealed nakedly how tiny was the British hold on the affections of the native peoples, not of India alone, but of the whole of South-east Asia.

The Indian Congress Party, however, hailed the results of the 1945 general election, congratulating the British on 'their abandonment of the old ideas and the acceptance of a new world'. Three members of the Labour Government had for many years been intimately interested in Indian problems: Attlee himself, Cripps, and Pethick Lawrence. Lord Mountbatten who succeeded Lord Wavell as Viceroy in March, 1947, revealed a brilliant grasp of Indian problems and aspirations. Yet the whole question was bedevilled by the tensions between the Hindu and Moslem communities. Attlee attempted to cut through the knot by declaring that Britain would definitely relinquish power in June, 1948. The immediate consequence was partition and bloodshed. But independent India and independent (Moslem) Pakistan opted to remain within the British Commonwealth, and India, under the Prime Ministership of Jawarhal Nehru, soon assumed a leading role in the counsels of the world.

The hasty concession of Indian independence roused bitter Conservative wrath, particularly on the part of Churchill himself, which, added to the controversies over Labour's domestic programme (the attempt to nationalize iron and steel, Churchill said, was 'a wanton act of party malice'), and legitimate disquiet over the economic crisis of 1947, suggests that party warfare was still at its most intense. In fact by 1950 the majority of the Conservative party had accepted the inviolability of the new social services and the new concept of

Commonwealth; there was in reality a large area of agreement, with a small spotlit arena in the centre in which the remaining issues were fought out with all the accoutrements and invective of party hostility. There was indeed some misgiving in Conservative quarters over Churchill's more extravagant utterances, which seemed to suggest that he was out of touch with the realities of the post-war world; 'A Liability?', *Picture Post* significantly asked in 1949 of the great war leader.

Where the traditional party pattern most clearly reasserted itself was in foreign politics: the bipartisanship here was in striking contrast to the bitter divides of the thirties. Certainly there remained a number of people on the extreme right in politics, and perhaps a fair proportion throughout the country as a whole, who were unprepared to face the one all-consuming consequence of the war; that there were now only two truly first-rank powers – America and Russia. British policy was inevitably dominated by the rivalries of these two giants, and particularly by the more obviously aggressionist tendencies manifested by Stalinist Russia after 1948. The trend of British foreign policy was towards close alignment with America and Western Europe, culminating in 1949 in the establishment of the North Atlantic Treaty Organization (NATO). The main criticisms of this trend came from the extreme left. The Government also had Conservative support, when, in 1947, it took the unprecedented step of introducing peace-time conscription. National Service, as we shall see in our final section, was to be a potent social factor in the lives of the post-war generation.

Many of the hopes vested in the United Nations Organization set up in 1945 remained unfulfilled in this condition of world division. (The division was symbolized by the economic, social, and political barrier between Eastern Europe, which fell under Soviet dominion, and Western Europe, known as the 'Iron Curtain'; the condition itself was termed the 'Cold War'.) Worse than this, a new shade fell across the world stage when in 1949 it became known that Russia as well as America had atomic weapons.

By 1950 the great fires of social change, greater even than those of 1906–1910, were dying low. Progressives like Edward Hulton or C. P. Snow's chronicle hero Lewis Eliot (see *Homecomings*) were disquieted by the realities of Labour Government. The most interesting literary-political phenomenon of all, not so much for what he wrote (*1984*, a thunderous satire of Stalinism, published just after his death in 1948), but for the reception he received, was George Orwell: as a critic of the left from the inside he had been ostracized by the only people in the thirties who had heard of him; as a public denunciator of the left he was now lionized by a wide popular readership. In the February general election Labour's total popular vote increased, but its majority, as with the Liberals in 1910, slumped: the figures were, Labour 315, Conservatives 297, Liberals 9. It rather looked as if society now wanted a period of consolidation. The impression was confirmed by the election of September, 1951, which brought the Conservatives back with 321 seats to Labour's 295; the Liberals now had a mere half-dozen.

CHAPTER FOURTEEN

THE AFFLUENT SOCIETY

THE social revolution brought both benefits and problems. The latter, if anything, were accentuated in the new decade. But on the whole the fifties are years of consolidation, in which nothing very dramatic is achieved, but in which the great changes of the immediate post-war years are allowed slowly to seep through society. It is now that the fruits (some of them sour) of extended educational opportunity, for instance, begin to make themselves clearly apparent.

The economy took no sharp change in direction when the Conservatives assumed power. Wherever possible the aim was to introduce some of the elasticity of private enterprise into the rigidities of State control. Thus the iron and steel industry was denationalized (though continued State supervision was vested in the Iron and Steel Board) and chunks of the road haulage industry were knocked down to private bidders; but that was about it. In 1950 after the outbreak of the Korean War the Labour Chancellor of the Exchequer, Hugh Gaitskell, faced with a greatly increased armaments expenditure, had departed from the principle of a totally free health service to the extent of levying a 50 per cent charge on spectacles and dentures. There was, therefore, no radical policy change implied in the cuts in the food subsidies imposed by the new Chancellor, R. A. Butler, in 1952. The gradual return to true peace-time conditions and, in particular, the turning of overseas trading terms in Britain's favour helped, however, towards a steady abandonment of rationing, finally achieved in 1954.

The continuity in Treasury policy, and the basic agreement

upon fundamentals among men of good will in all parties was expressed in a new coinage of the time, 'Butskellism'. As, however, the Government denied to itself many of the overall planning controls which Labour had used, it found itself relying more and more on purely monetary control. Its stock remedy whenever the economy seemed to be getting out of hand was to raise the Bank Rate. Sensible enough within its limits, this dear money policy tended to discourage expansion. The broad economic picture seemed to be one of fits and starts; the economy seemed to be losing its dynamism, and this indeed was reflected in a slackening in the growth of total productivity.

But undoubtedly there was over the whole decade a striking increase in the wealth of the community. The expense-account business class flourished; extravagant private building, new shop frontages, and so on, were everywhere to be seen. But conspicuous consumption was not confined to one class alone. With a high level of industrial demand, wage-packets generally were unprecedentedly large; between 1951 and 1958 the average real earnings of the industrial worker increased by 20 per cent. Cars, washing-machines, refrigerators, came within the reach of ordinary families. By 1959 30 per cent of the people owned or were buying their own homes. It is in the curious combination of the lack of dynamism in the economy as a whole, and obvious private affluence, that the basis of the 'I'm all right, Jack' atmosphere which characterizes an important part of British life in the fifties, is to be found.

Trade union co-operation with the Government was encouraged for at least the first half of the period under review. In the later years sporadic militance began to appear on both sides. The interlude of tough Treasury policy associated with Mr Peter Thorneycroft soon passed, but on the other side the persistence of 'wildcat' strikes became a cause for concern to the whole community. That the desire of the Conservative traditionalists to cripple the unions by legislative means was now out of the question was finally demonstrated by the Conservative Party Conference of 1961. For the period

1950–60 as a whole the atmosphere was one of political quietude.

Winston Churchill was seventy-seven when he returned to office in 1951. Although there had been some doubts as to his adaptability to the new political and social environment, his Government contained men with a fine liberal record like R. A. Butler, and Harold Macmillan (who was Minister of Housing), and Sir Walter Monckton as Minister of Labour was progressive and conciliatory. Churchill, of course, brought with him his own great personal prestige; he looked, and sounded, the part. This was, indeed, a Government of the country's traditional rulers (Macmillan, after all, was married to a daughter of the Duke of Devonshire) adapted to modern conditions. Churchill had four co-ordinating ministers – nick-named the 'overlords' – all in the House of Lords. One of them was Lord Cherwell, the first professional scientist to hold Cabinet office. The return of the top people to the top helps to explain the fog of indifference which now dropped over politics.

The Conservatives presented a shining image backed by an apparent party unity. Far other was the case of the late governing party. Gaitskell's Health Service charges in 1950 had provoked the resignations of Aneurin Bevan, the architect of the free Health Service, Harold Wilson, the President of the Board of Trade, and John Freeman, soon to forsake the Treasury Bench altogether for the silvery screen. The differences, it transpired, were on the wider issue of Britain's colossally expensive defence policy. The original theory behind this had been that Britain and the West should so strengthen their offensive power that they should be in a position to 'deter' Russia, and to 'negotiate from strength'. Unfortunately it had become clear by the fifties that, if anything, Russia had the greater offensive power. The original policy had, perforce, to be altered to one of mad scramble to keep up with Russia. This policy the left in the Labour party opposed, mainly for emotional reasons, though Bevan himself argued on the grounds that it was fruitlessly crippling the economy. Friction between left and right in the Labour party had existed ever since the party was founded in 1900; but never before had the left had a leader of the stature of Bevan; hence the seriousness of the 'Bevanite' movement, a seriousness exacerbated by the succession to the leadership of Gaitskell, who was much more firmly identified with the right than Attlee, always the consummate chairman, ever had been. To the electorate Labour presented a picture of warring unfitness for government.

Indifference showed itself in the general election held in May, 1955, by Sir Anthony Eden, shortly after he succeeded Churchill as Prime Minister; the percentage of the electorate who troubled to go to the polls declined from 82·6 in 1951 to 76·8. But there could be no doubt as to the widespread contentment with the Conservative record: for the first time under modern conditions the party in office increased its strength. The final figures were: Conservatives, 319; Labour, 277; Liberals, 6. After a further spell of office, during which Macmillan replaced the ailing Eden, the Conservatives completed a unique hat-trick. The election of October, 1959, produced the following results: Conservatives, 365; Labour, 258; Liberals, 6; Independent, 1. The Conservatives had again increased their strength. What is more, the percentage of the electorate voting had gone up to 78·7.

In 1959 the Conservative policy of introducing as much economic freedom as possible within the broadly collectivist framework was enjoying its greatest successes. Although there were small local pockets of unemployment – the cotton industry had been in trouble since 1952, and some of the old distressed areas, the Clyde, in particular, were beginning to nag again – and the coal mines were now producing too much coal and the railways not carrying enough passengers, the party in power was able to campaign boldly on the slogan 'You've Never Had It So Good'. Labour still seemed too divided within itself to be capable of efficient rule; there was also the feeling that it was not really so very different in essence from the Conservatives – only less successful. Certainly the number of trade unionists in the Parliamentary Labour Party was dropping, the number of products of Oxbridge increasing. A labour M.P., Fred Lee, commented in 1954:

If this tendency continues we shall find that the Parliamentary Party has become a middle-class organization which strives desperately to prove its connexions with the working class by displaying its few remaining trade union products with all the enthusiasm of a child with an unusual toy.

The Yorkshire hero of John Braine's *Room at the Top* remarks that he never sees his Labour M.P., who lives in Hampstead.

This is all of a piece with the return to the classic norm of political Tweedledum and Tweedledee, or of Ins and Outs, save that Labour looked like being permanently out. From the right Evelyn Waugh was heard to complain that the Conservatives had not put the clock back by one minute. The finest satire of the political situation appeared in Edward Hyams's *Gentian Violet* (1953), in which the hero is elected to Parliament as *both* a Conservative *and* a Socialist. James Blundell had both retained his links with his humble origins and, by means of a distinguished war career (an important social phenomenon), had attained the social status signalized by the adoption of the name James Stewart-Blundell. It was in the latter persona that he was elected Conservative M.P. for a rural commuterland constituency; it was as plain Jim Blundell that he was subsequently elected Labour M.P. for an industrial area north of London. Blundell expected instant exposure in the House of Commons, but he found:

Nobody noticed anybody else. . . . A member might be on his feet talking away yet boring nobody, as nobody was obliged to listen . . . it reduced the most ambitious and domineering public men to the status of mere prefects, with certain privileges, like putting their feet on the table. . . If democracy was to be found anywhere, Jim felt, it was here in the House of Commons.

And Jim soon began to be very proud of being two members of it.

Maurice Edelman (himself a Labour M.P.) is a kindlier commentator in his two important domestic political novels, *Who Goes Home?* (1956) and *The Minister* (1961). In both the Government in power is clearly Conservative, but there is no sense of strong socio-political clash; here we have clearly a game of Ins and Outs, played on both sides by, on the whole, men of good will – the problems tend to be human and personal rather than political and social. *Who Goes Home?* concerns a Cabinet Minister, Erskine, whose whole political career is thrown in jeopardy by a trivial indiscretion committed in America: in the interests of political purity his own Prime Minister is prepared to sacrifice him, but he is saved by the intervention of the Leader of the Opposition – the atmosphere of all basically good chaps together could not be taken further. The political kernel of *The Minister* concerns an African colony which is about to attain self-government – sensibly enough since, in the absence of clear-cut domestic issues, Britain's relationship with the emergent African nationalism was one of the key political problems of the age. Writers, such as Walter Allen (in *All in a Lifetime*) or Frank Tilsley (in *The Voice of the Crowd*), who wished to base their novels upon actual political strife had to forsake the present for the stirring days earlier in the century when the Labour movement was still on the march.

'Apathy' was a word much on people's lips. Yet there was incident enough in the second half of the decade to disturb the eighteenth-century quality of public life. In 1956 the Government of Sir Anthony Eden, apparently entertaining exaggerated notions as to the importance of the Egyptian dictator Colonel Nasser, took the opportunity provided by an Israeli attack on Egypt (for which there was some justification) of joining the invasion, in collaboration with the French. This clear betrayal of the principles of the United Nations aroused a storm throughout the country, among Conservatives as well as Socialists; though it was maintained, probably with justice, that many Labour supporters welcomed this last fling of British jingoism, at least until the whole Suez venture teetered to an ignominious close. Eden, genuinely a very sick man, resigned some months later, and Harold Macmillan, the eager young man of earlier days pretty thoroughly concealed in a veneer of Edwardian unflappability, took over.

Beyond the affluence and the apathy a giant sore thumb stuck out. Since 1952 both Russia and America had been testing the hydrogen bomb, effectively guaranteeing that if war should break out civilization would be destroyed. After 1955 Britain began testing her own H-bomb. A new political movement whose object was the British renunciation of nuclear weapons sprang into being. With its organized marches and demonstrations, the Campaign for Unilateral Nuclear Disarmament, based firmly in the student population of the community but drawing in housewives and ordinary people from all walks of life, was an important sign that a healthy concern with the large issues of the day was not yet dead. Indeed one can see on this question a return among many of the younger artists and poets to something like the commitment of the thirties. The motivation behind the campaign was confused. It reached its climax in 1960 when it captured the Labour Party Conference, but was thrust out into the cold again the following year. However sound or unsound its arguments, however successful or unsuccessful, the movement was of importance in dramatizing the fundamental issue which now hung over British society.

Though Britain had long led the world in the practical exposition of progressive doctrines, she was now falling sadly behind the times. Capital punishment – which to many seemed an obscene barbarity – was still preserved despite the absence of any rational evidence in its favour. Despite the recommendation of the Wolfenden Report of 1957 that 'homosexual behaviour between consenting adults in private should no longer be a criminal offence' it continued to be a criminal offence. The prison system remained in essence retributive rather than regenerative. Finally there were grounds for criticizing the whole ethos of the affluent society, more especially since rising living standards for the pampered majority meant very real hardship for the neglected minority, especially old age pensioners.

Overseas, the avowed aim of the Government was to assist Britain's remaining African possessions towards self-determination: in an utterance which for eloquent quotability ranks with some of those of Churchill, Mr Macmillan in January, 1960, while in South Africa, referred to the 'wind of change' blowing through the African continent. But the Government ran into difficulties with the white settler class in Centra Africa, and despite the best efforts of the liberal and able Colonial Secretary, Mr Iain Macleod, the suspicion grew that the Government had too many ties of blood and loyalty with this class to be able to allow full scope to African aspirations. Significance was attached to the fact that Mr Macleod left the Colonial Office in October 1961. The failure of the Government to dissociate itself from the Fascist régime in Spain and the Salazar dictatorship in Portugal also aroused criticism.

There was then a sufficiency of rallying points for radical sentiment. The question was, could this sentiment find an adequate outlet in the Labour party. There was a *prima facie* case for arguing that the Labour party was a spent force; that it was now a victim of the same sort of long-term sociological trends as had stifled the Liberal party earlier in the century. Public opinion polls showed that more and more people were regarding themselves as middle class, so that a party which sought to base itself on 'labour' as a class could expect to find its support dwindling. This is the context in which the revival of Liberalism, very apparent in by-elections, scarcely perceptible in the more realistic test of general elections, should be placed. By 1961 the political picture had not resolved itself. Certainly political apathy seemed at least to be thawing in face of the new revival of radicalism. The Conservative party itself seemed set on maintaining a new progressive image, and Mr Macleod emerged as Mr Macmillan's heir apparent.

Below the surface of party politics more fundamental changes were taking place in the balance of power within society. First let us refer again to the ever-increasing demand for trained scientists, reflected, to take a random example, in the following typical statistics from a school in Bolton: for the five-year period 1935–9 there was an aggregate registration of 29 pupils in arts, 32 in science; for 1955–9 the comparable figures are 157 and 620 respectively. Not only were more scientists being produced but most of these scientists were going straight into practical work for industry or, perhaps, the State. D. S. L. Cardwell (*The Organization of Science in England* (1957) pp. 177–8) estimated the number of research and industrial chemists in England to be about 10,000. He reckoned the total number engaged in all forms of teaching as only a little over half of this figure. 'Industry', he concludes, 'has replaced teaching as an occupation of the natural scientists'. Though he would probably not have approved of all of these developments, one important suggestion made by F. G. Hopkins in the thirties was taken up: there was now, in the person of Lord Hailsham, a Minister of Science.

An utterly different element in the complex of British society was much in evidence in the 1950's. The coronation of Queen Elizabeth in 1953 was celebrated with at least as much pomp and popular rejoicing as the 1937 occasion. In 1957 three people in five throughout the country confessed to still having in their possession souvenirs of the 1953 coronation.

The Crown was still more than a public show piece. When Sir Anthony Eden resigned in January, 1957, the most obvious candidate for the Prime Ministership seemed to be R. A. Butler. In the last analysis the actual choice of Harold Macmillan was that of the Queen, acting, of course, on advice; in this case the advice of Churchill and Lord Salisbury, the *eminence grise* of modern Conservatism.

Tory peers, the Press, civil servants, managers, the Crown politicians, pomp and ceremony: where exactly were the levers of power in modern society? It is not surprising that in the later fifties the somewhat vague concept of 'The Establishment' became a commonplace. (The word had actually been coined forty years before by the novelist, Ford Madox Ford.) The most significant literary commentator on the new 'corridors of power' (his own phrase) in society was C. P. Snow. While Galsworthy in the twenties had still felt it worthwhile to describe the doings of the old Victorian propertied class, Snow in the forties and fifties was preoccupied with the scientists and managers of the civil service and private industry.

CHAPTER FIFTEEN

THE DECADE OF DETACHMENT

ONE section of the community, comprising some of the beneficiaries of the extension of educational opportunity, found itself rather at a loss in the society of the fifties. Young men, usually from a lower middle-class background, found after acquiring a degree (usually from a provincial university) and some experience of the world from National Service, that there were few jobs in which they could fully deploy their talents or earn more money than their contemporaries who had left school at fifteen.

This predicament was explored in John Wain's novel, *Hurry on Down* (1954), whose protagonist, Charles Lumley, makes his fortune by disowning his academic qualifications and settling for a policy of dishonesty. Spineless, complex-ridden versions of the same character appeared in Kingsley Amis's *Lucky Jim* (1954) and *That Uncertain Feeling* (1955). Jim Dixon is a University tutor, too aggrieved at his miserable salary (as far as one can make out) to do any work, or show any interest at all in any slightest aspect of his duties; *luckily* a wealthy business man recognizes his sterling qualities and he is whisked off to better things and a prosperous marriage. The hero of the second book is an underpaid librarian, who after describing at inordinate length the exteriors and interiors of other people's big cars (the modish – then – steering-column gear change fascinated him), finally settles for his own dull marriage with his own boring wife. Beyond making explicit the dilemmas of the angry young man, these important novels breathe the atmosphere of a whole social malaise: covetousness.

Jimmy Porter in John Osborne's play *Look Back in Anger* (first produced in 1956), and Joe Lampton in John Braine's

Room at the Top were both made of sterner stuff. Set against a realistic Yorkshire background, Joe Lampton's career again illustrates that in the windfall state, a position at the top is to be attained by talents other than those born of education. Osborne's anger, in *Look Back in Anger*, in *The Entertainer* and in his unsuccessful musical *The World of Paul Slickey*, is much less personal and goes wider and deeper. Osborne came nearer than anyone else to developing a coherent criticism of the age as a whole. Consequently he attained a certain notoriety, assisted by his own occasional outbursts and sedulously fostered by a section of the Press.

Anger was not confined to a small and (though they did not think so) privileged element of the community. Much attention was focused upon youth, its destructiveness and its addiction to speed and the possession of a motor-bicycle. Many social commentators described the leather-clad gangs which congregated at roadside cafés, ferociously revving their engines. Simon Raven, the novelist, reported an interesting conversation in an article in the *Spectator*, 27th October, 1961):

The young knights do not often enter pubs, but a small group of them had just come and gone, they had drunk one soft drink apiece, still wearing their helmets, and then they had looked at each other in silence and left – without returning their glasses to the bar.

'They're disappointed, see?' croaked the woman (landlady? barmaid? casual help?).

'Why?' I said.

'Because they've been told that they're important and they've found out that they're not.'

'I don't quite follow you. I should have thought these days –'

'Yes, dear, of course you would. And so did they. Education for a start – everything, they were told, is going to be done for Youth. Nothing too good for them – the country's Youth. And then, advertisements and so on. "Special for you." "Ready now for you." As though the man on the screen meant *you yourself*, not just one more of a million suckers. All this stuff – whether it's put out by the Government or the telly – they've thought it applied to them personally!'

'Well, they don't do too badly at that. Good money . . .'

'Yes, dear. Good money, easy hours, plenty of welfare – the lot. But none of that individual importance they thought they were promised. Just one of a crowd. Doing a dull job that anybody else could do at a moment's notice. Nothing "special for you" about that.'

'So they buy these motor-bikes to make up?'

'That's it. . . . Make a lot of noise . . . assert themselves.'

'Then why don't they go somewhere worth while on them? Why just hang around the streets?'

'Girls.'

'They could find girls anywhere.'

'Plenty here. I told you, dear. They don't buy those bloody bikes to go anywhere, only to kick up a row so that people will look at them and they can think themselves important like their teachers and the telly always said they were. Get it? And of course the girls look at them too, and there they are' . . .

'So they pick up the girls and then tumble them in the sand-dunes?'

'A few perhaps.' The woman shrugged: 'But mostly they just marry them.'

'They what?'

'Marry them. Once you see one of those boys with a girl on his pillion, you know the end is near for him. In six months he'll have sold his beautiful bike and got a scooter to go to work on. If that. He'll have settled, see?'

'But why? If they're trying to assert their independence . . . to get attention . . .'

'That's just the way to get attention. From the girls for a start. And then you know what a fuss people always make about engaged couples, young love, newly-weds. It's ordinary enough, but it gets attention – for a time anyhow. Tears at the wedding, lots of free care at the maternity clinic. That's why they all marry so young nowadays. They think they're doing something original, something important, and so the telly advertisements – "Special for *you*" – start to mean something again.'

Teenage immorality was given a great deal of attention in the Press and on television; there was a clear increase in the number of unmarried mothers of youthful years. The basic fact was that with the expansion of welfare services, better feeding, better housing, the population of the country was maturing at a much earlier age. The new teenage paradox thrown up by social change was that of a sector of society physically adult, but legally, socially and politically under age. The problem was intensified by the massive spending power now commanded by this sector, which resulted in it being subjected to an advertising bombardment in which most of the shot involved some form of sexual suggestiveness. The promiscuity of coffee-bar, jive-cellar and jazz festival was not different in character from the gay irresponsibility of fashionable society in the twenties – it had simply moved to a different social class. Religious belief and the Victorian code of restraints associated with it had long since, we have seen, received its damaging blows. The question now was not so much one of further religious decline, but simply of expansion of opportunity.

There were, in fact, grounds for believing that the post-war generation took a turn back towards traditional moral canons, in some sense, perhaps, as a reaction against the relaxed standards of the inter-war years. This at any rate was the convincing theme of Doris Lessing's novel *Retreat to Innocence*. Economic prosperity too, as J. Mogey has pointed out in *The Family and Neighbourhood*, fostered the idea of the family as a basic social unit. Marriage seemed a most popular institution, embarked upon at a much earlier stage in life than previous generations would have thought proper. The great popular idols were no longer Errol Flynns with wicked, wicked ways, but guitar-clutching youths happily married at nineteen. The 'knights' described in the *Spectator* article quoted above had, we have seen, more than one point in common with the heroes of the Kingsley Amis novels, and even, indeed, with Jimmy Porter: all are publicists for marriage.

We have had no occasion to refer to the post-1940 fashion world. Wartime and post-war austerity did not encourage innovation. The post-war 'New Look' was hailed more as a sign of a break in the grey clouds than for any aesthetic appeal. Wartime scarcity had encouraged the production of men's trousers without turn-ups: this the conservative British male had circumvented simply by buying a size too large and having his own turn-ups made out of the excess. Where forties' scarcity failed fifties' fashion succeeded. Men's trousers became slimmer and the turn-up tended to disappear. In the early fifties they were accompanied by a lengthened jacket, so that the whole ensemble presented a definitely Edwardian appearance. (Some linguistic genius coined the phrase 'Teddy boys' to describe the street corner youths who sported an exaggerated version of this style complete with long hair and pointed shoes.) Later, jackets took on a shorter, boxed, Italian shape, for the late fifties underwent a passion for all things Italian, unknown since the heyday of the Italian landscape in the eighteenth century. Milan and Rome assumed the place in British life traditionally associated with Paris. In 1959 Austin produced a Farina line car; Zefferelli mounted production of *Cav* and *Pag* at Covent Garden, *Romeo and Juliet* at the old Vic, and *Othello* at Stratford-on-Avon.

Till women asserted a jealous sartorial supremacy in the mid-nineteenth century man had always been the social peacock. There was now something of a revival of interest in men's clothes. Arthur Seaton, the factory-hand hero of Alan Sillitoe's novel *Saturday Night and Sunday Morning* (1958), boasts a wardrobe full of twenty-guinea suits. Women, of course, were in no sense outshone. There was a general return to the styles associated with the twenties, and skirt lengths became appreciably shorter. There was a great boom in the type of multiple store which specialized in the sale of fashionable and colourful clothing at low prices; the consequence was that the appearance at least of the country's female population was shot through with a welcome gaiety and zest. Not, however, that the effect was quite universal: the women, of Aberdeen, for instance (see controversy in the local Press, 1960), looked drab compared with those of London or even, say, Edinburgh. Manufacturers boomed more loudly and more publicly than ever before the virtues of the latest advances in foundation garments: never, it appeared, could so many shapes be assumed by so many women with so little effort.

Old traditions remained. With affluence, beer consumption rose – 12 per cent up on pre-war – but 'the pub still persists as a social institution' (T. Harrisson: *Britain Revisited* (1961, p. 194). However, greater wealth, ease of living, standardization of clothing, could not fail to facilitate the transition, literally and metaphorically, from public bar to lounge bar, and to open the horizons beyond. A hundred years before, Thomas Cook had set the Victorian bourgeoisie off on trips to Europe; now travel agencies were to be found everywhere, escorting people of all sorts to all parts of the world. Chinese and Indian restaurants began to appear in provincial towns. The most striking catering phenomenon was the success of the far from cheap but completely classless establishments ('Corner House', 'Grill and Griddle', or what have you) usually associated with the giant catering firms of Lyons or Fortes. Social strains, then, were easing out, save perhaps among those at the bottom of the old middle-class who saw their status threatened.

But a new and dangerous social strain forced itself on the attention of the public in the outburst of ugly racial rioting in Notting Hill in West London in 1958. The flow of coloured immigrants, particularly from the West Indies, increased all through the decade: from Jamaica the affluent society appeared to have milk and honey and to spare. This flow reacted with Britain's other chronic social ill: inadequate housing. The immigrants perforce congregated in the slummiest areas. The problem offered no easy solution, but many people became uneasily aware that if Britain had no *apartheid*, no segregation, she seemed to have a colour bar. In 1961 the Government announced legislation designed to restrict the inflow of coloured immigrants.

The colour bar provided a theme for some earnest and often rather dull television plays. Social comment, too, we have noted, was an important element in the most characteristic novels of the period. Comment, but not commitment. This was, indeed, apart possibly from a few hints in a contrary direction about 1960, a decade of detachment. The sense of detachment was at its most profound in the plays of Samuel Beckett and Harold Pinter, who explored, respectively, the desolation and the hidden dreads of humanity.

Pinter's first play, *The Birthday Party*, was killed by the critics; but he achieved fame with *The Caretaker*. This illustrates well one of the less admirable features of the times. There seemed to be only two possibilities in front of the writer: either he remained spurned and unknown, or else he achieved a much inflated reputation and substantial royalties on the basis of one work alone. This happened with Osborne, Braine, and with a young playwright from Salford, Shelagh Delaney, whose *A Taste of Honey* (in fact a highly poetic work) enjoyed something of a *succès de scandale*. This was all in keeping with the ethos of the windfall state, and was an aspect of the centralizing, simplifying tendency which accompanied the growth of mass communications: it was easier to publicize one or two big names than to explore the merits of a host of lesser ones. Yet it would also be true to say that never before had fewer men of talent starved in garrets. Arts Council grants, University Fellowships, hack work for television, all helped to ensure that the budding genius could at least keep body and soul together. In a survey entitled *Art lies Bleeding*, Francis Walter had discovered that in 1937 a successful artist had a *minus* income of ten pounds per annum (the cost of his overheads being higher by that amount than the value of his sales); now a reasonably successful artist could count on netting perhaps a hundred pounds a year. Not a princely sum, but a sign of change.

It is to mass communications that we must now again turn. The crucial event was the breaking in 1954 of the BBC's monopoly of television broadcasting, which had enjoyed a very rapid growth since the war. The Television Act of that year permitted the introduction of an alternative 'Independent' Television Service, to be financed from advertising revenue. This, it was widely argued, led inevitably to a general lowering of standards. Yet it would be stupid to deny that both television channels did at times put on programmes of very high quality, which showed that television, carefully handled, could be a great force of enlightenment. Current events could be presented with a dramatic force not possible in the newspaper Press. Snatches at least of opera and ballet were brought into the home.

The rise of television and the increased glitter, if not richness, of life generally had an adverse effect on cinema attendances. From the peak figure of 31 millions per week in 1946 there was a steady decline all through the fifties and into the sixties. Yet it was in the late fifties that Britain for the first time produced a number of films of truly international calibre; films such as *Room at the Top*, *I'm All Right, Jack* and *The Entertainer*.

We have said nothing so far of the gramophone record industry, which in actual fact was launched in the United States as long ago as the late nineteenth century. The really spectacular technical advances did not come till the late forties, when the long-playing record was developed. On its first appearance in Britain the long-playing gramophone record was the prerogative of the highly musically conscious few. But the rise of the Record Clubs supplying the popular classics at greatly reduced prices suggested that the circle was widening. This was borne out by the trend of over-the-counter sales. At the same time there was a mammoth and ever-growing sale for Americanized pop music. The dual trend is continuing: greater trivialization on the one hand, yet growing opportunity for cultural expansion on the other.

Compare, then, the opportunities, the attitudes, the health of the man in the street gleefully expecting a short sharp defeat of Germany in 1914, with those of his counterpart today. No doubt as to the explosion which has taken place in British society, even if it is an explosion which has brought its own proportion of harmful fall-out.

CONCLUSION: CHANGES OF WIND,
1962–63

THIS book began with a reflection on the dangers of looking for watersheds, or even turning-points, in history. The danger increases as one approaches the present. None the less a few tentative remarks about Britain at the beginning of 1963 will be attempted here.

The period since 1951 has been described as one of consolidation. While there was a movement to free the country from the more extreme restrictions and controls felt to be out of place in peace-time, so that planning fell out of fashion, there was all-party acceptance of the Welfare State and full employment economy. Furthermore, by the later fifties the full benefits of the social developments discussed throughout the course of this book, were being reaped by all classes.

The Conservatives had gained in strength in three successive elections. Under their rule the country (apart from the ill-fated Suez venture) had adjusted itself remarkably well to a changed world situation in which Britain was no longer mistress of important territories overseas, and no longer, in comparison with the giants, Russia and America, a first-rank power. To this changed world situation the countries of Western Europe had reacted in their own way. From the setting up in 1951 of the European Coal and Steel Community (which Britain refused to join) there was a steady movement towards economic and, eventually, it was hoped, political union; a united Western Europe, its sponsors believed, would in power and influence stand comparison with the world giants. The first major concrete expression of this movement was the European Common Market, established by the Treaties of Rome, of March, 1957.

At first only the Liberals were in favour of British

participation in this experiment. But as the economic potential of the Common Market became more and more apparent, Britain, in late 1959, took the leading role in creating a European Free Trade Area of those peripheral countries (Norway and Portugal, for instance) who were not members of the Common Market. In July, 1961, she began tentative negotiations for entry into the Common Market itself; the main point at issue was the extent to which membership would imperil existing connexions with the Commonwealth.

An added motive for seeking entry to the Common Market was the economic stagnation from which Britain was clearly suffering; it was argued that free competition from Europe would blow away the cobwebs of restrictive practices and out-dated business methods, said to encrust British industry. In 1961, the Chancellor of the Exchequer, Mr Selwyn Lloyd, began an attack on the problem of inflation, particularly serious in a time of stagnation, by the institution of a 'Wages Pause'. Observed only in the small sector of the community over whose incomes the Government had direct control, and scarcely at all in private industry, this policy was neither fair nor effective. Thus in the Spring of 1962, the Government announced its conversion back to the ideas of economic planning: the Prime Minister had perhaps been reading the words of his youth quoted at the beginning of Chapter Eight.

The attempt to return to expansionist policies was signalized by the replacement in June, 1962, of Mr Selwyn Lloyd by Mr Reginald Maudling. New economic initiatives seemed more than ever essential with the collapse of the Common Market negotiations in January, 1963. But the tares sown in the fifties had taken deep root, and in January, 1963, the Government found itself faced with an unemployment total of 800,000. The problem had by no means attained the dimensions of that which we examined when discussing the twenties and thirties, but once again, ominously, it was the old depressed areas of the north and Scotland which were bearing the brunt of it: 'consolidation' was beginning to look a little like 'regression'.

A number of incidents between January, 1962, and January,

1963, cast a revealing light on the latest shaping of the forces we have traced throughout this book. In its announcements of a new hospital building programme, a slum clearance drive, and an increase in unemployment insurance benefits, the Government showed its awareness that the physical snags (see above, pp. 114–118) concealed in the burst of collectivist legislation of the forties, were becoming a serious threat to the Welfare State itself. The Pilkington Committee on Television, publishing their findings in June, preached an excoriating sermon on the social failings of commercialized mass communications. In the world at large, the Cuban crisis of October, 1962, made it finally and ruthlessly clear that the destiny of human civilization, which Britain had sought manfully, and on the whole honourably, to influence in two world wars, was now quite out of British hands.

The year 1962 presented a picture of self-examination not unlike that of the thirties, a self-examination which was intensified by the difficulties and doubts attending upon our arduous and unsuccessful negotiations with the Common Market countries. Economic failure, inconsistency, and apparent lack of leadership, brought strong discontent with Conservative administration, and in a series of by-elections throughout the year, the Government vote slumped, to the advantage of both Labour (itself cruelly hit by the tragic death of Mr Hugh Gaitskell in January, 1963) and Liberal. Take all these points, add the stirrings of radicalism and even commitment which began to appear in the late fifties, and we might predict that the period of consolidation is now drawing to a close, and that British society may be about to embark upon a further period of change.

INDEX